Steck-Vaughn

GED

LANGUAGE ARTS, READING
Exercise Book

STECK-VAUGHN
ELEMENTARY · SECONDARY · ADULT · LIBRARY
A Harcourt Company

ACKNOWLEDGMENTS

Executive Editor: Ellen Northcutt
Senior Editor: Donna Townsend
Associate Design Director: Joyce Spicer
Supervising Designer: Pamela Heaney

Photo Credits: Cover: (old books) ©Strauss/Curtis/The Stock Market, (open books) ©Telegraph Colour Library/FPG International; p.i. ©Telegraph Colour Library/FPG International.

Literary Credits: Acknowledgments for literary selections are on pages 107 and 108, which are an extension of this copyright page.

ISBN 0-7398-3604-8

Copyright © 2002 Steck-Vaughn Company

Printed in the United States of America.

6 7 8 9 10 RP 07 06 05 04 03 02

Contents

The *Steck-Vaughn GED Language Arts, Reading Exercise Book* provides you with review and practice in answering the types of questions found on the actual GED Language Arts, Reading Test. It can be used with *Steck-Vaughn GED Language Arts, Reading, Steck-Vaughn Complete GED Preparation,* or other appropriate materials. This book has two sections: practice exercises and simulated tests.

Practice Exercises

The practice exercises are divided into four units: nonfiction, fiction, poetry, and drama. The nonfiction unit includes general nonfiction selections, reviews about visual texts or viewing, and business documents. The fiction unit contains passages from literary works written during three time periods: before 1920, from 1920–1960, and after 1960. The poetry unit contains full-length poems of various types, and the drama unit contains excerpts from a variety of plays. Each unit provides practice in answering questions about literary selections similar to those you will find on the GED Test.

Simulated Tests

This exercise book contains two full-length Simulated GED Language Arts, Reading Tests. Each Simulated Test has the same number of items as the actual GED Test and provides practice with types of items similar to those on the GED Test. The Simulated Tests can help you decide if you are ready to take the GED Language Arts, Reading Test.

To get the most benefit from the Simulated Test section, take each test under the same time restrictions as for the actual GED Test. For each test, complete the 40 items within 65 minutes. Space the two examinations apart by at least a week.

Reading Passages   The reading passages are always introduced with a question to help guide your thinking about the passage. On the test, 75% of the passages are literary selections (fiction, poetry, and drama) and 25% are nonfiction selections. When you are reading a drama passage, be sure to read the stage directions carefully. Poems are usually relatively short, but take time to think about and understand the poem. Rereading the poem entirely may be helpful.

The GED Language Arts, Reading Test examines your ability to understand, apply, analyze, and evaluate information in a variety of literary and nonfiction texts.

All of the questions on the GED Language Arts, Reading Test are multiple choice. You will not be tested on your knowledge of specific literary works or authors, but rather on your ability to understand, interpret, and analyze what you read.

Following is an explanation of the four types of questions that you will practice in this book and that are found on the GED Language Arts, Reading Test.

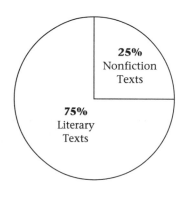

25% Nonfiction Texts

75% Literary Texts

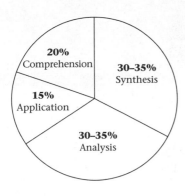

20% Comprehension

30–35% Synthesis

15% Application

30–35% Analysis

1. Comprehension: These questions require you to restate information, summarize the main idea, and explain the meaning of the passage. Twenty percent of the questions on the GED Test are comprehension questions.

2. Application: These questions ask you to apply information or ideas to situations that differ from the one in the passage. You must be able to transfer concepts and principles from the reading to a new context. Fifteen percent of the questions on the GED Test are application questions.

3. Analysis: For these questions you need to draw conclusions and make inferences from the information given in the passage. You must also be able to identify elements of style and structure, identify the effects produced by different techniques, recognize cause and effect relationships, and recognize unstated assumptions. Thirty to thirty-five percent of the questions on the GED Test are analysis questions.

4. Synthesis: These types of questions ask you to interpret the overall structure, characterization, tone, point of view, style, or purpose of a passage. They may also ask you to compare and contrast elements within the passage or to integrate information from outside the passage with information in it (expanded synthesis). Thirty to thirty-five percent of the questions on the GED Test are synthesis questions.

Analysis of Performance Charts

After each Simulated Test, an Analysis of Performance Chart will help you determine if you are ready to take the GED Language Arts, Reading Test. The charts give a breakdown by content area and by question type. By completing these charts, you can determine your own strengths and weaknesses as they relate to the areas tested in reading.

Answers and Explanations

The Answers and Explanations section gives explanations of why an answer is correct and why the other answer choices are incorrect. Sometimes by studying the reason an answer is incorrect, you can learn to avoid a similar error in the future. Each question is also identified by question type: comprehension, application, analysis, or synthesis.

Correlation Chart

The following chart shows how the sections of this exercise book relate to sections of other Steck-Vaughn GED preparation books. Refer to these books for further instruction or review.

CONTENT AREAS	Nonfiction	Fiction	Poetry	Drama
BOOK TITLES *Steck-Vaughn GED Language Arts, Reading Exercise Book*	Unit 1	Unit 2	Unit 3	Unit 4
Steck-Vaughn GED Language Arts, Reading	Unit 1	Unit 2	Unit 3	Unit 4
Steck-Vaughn Complete GED Preparation	Unit 5, Nonfiction	Unit 5, Fiction	Unit 5, Poetry	Unit 5, Drama

General Nonfiction

Directions: Choose the one best answer to each question.

Questions 1 through 4 refer to the following excerpt from a biography.

HOW CAN HE EVER WIN?

What had changed in America to lead Marshall and his impecunious little band of lawyers to think that they could reverse the tide of segregation in America? How
(5) audacious of this black man and his allies to think they could alter the legal landscape of America!

"I have to keep believing, because I know our cause is right. Justice and
(10) reason are on our side. Everybody knows this but those enslaved to customs that say whites are whites and Negroes are Negroes and never the twain shall meet. But I tell you, it isn't easy knowing that
(15) we'll be going up against the most renowned constitutional lawyer in American history," said Marshall.

Governor Byrnes of South Carolina had pleaded with John William Davis to
(20) argue the South's case for maintaining Jim Crow schools. Byrnes had persuaded Davis to "defend the South" for just a silver tea service—and to satisfy his personal support for "states' rights" and his
(25) conviction that race was just a reality of life that could be reflected in statutes.

While Marshall respected his foe—he had cut classes while in law school to watch the brilliance of Davis's
(30) arguments—he knew that he had a few advantages of his own. He had, in a short period, won thirteen cases before the Supreme Court while losing two. Years earlier, he had enjoyed the heady
(35) compliment of seeing three robed judges of the Fourth Circuit Court of Appeals step off the bench to congratulate him on his successful argument that Virginia had to pay black teachers the same salaries that
(40) it paid white teachers.

I left Marshall that fall day of '53 thinking that he believed in himself and his cause so much that it was impossible for me and others not to believe in him.

Carl T. Rowan, *Dream Makers, Dream Breakers, The World of Justice Thurgood Marshall*

1. Based on the first paragraph of the excerpt, which statement best describes the writer's belief about the upcoming case?

    (1) The odds favored Marshall.
    (2) The odds were against Marshall.
    (3) Marshall had no chance of winning.
    (4) Marshall was sure to win.
    (5) Both sides had equal chances.

2. When Marshall was congratulated by the three judges, he had argued a case to end which of the following?

    (1) slavery in America
    (2) segregated schools in the South
    (3) racial inequality for blacks
    (4) unequal pay for black teachers
    (5) states' rights

3. Which of the following best describes Marshall's attitude toward John William Davis?

    (1) contempt
    (2) fear
    (3) anger
    (4) little respect
    (5) great respect

4. What caused the writer to believe in Marshall's chance to win the school segregation case?

    (1) Davis's legal expertise
    (2) Marshall's associates
    (3) Marshall's belief in himself and his cause
    (4) Marshall's success in law school
    (5) the role of Governor Byrnes

WHAT WASN'T OBVIOUS TO THE AUDIENCE?

Early in this century, a horse named Hans amazed the people of Berlin by his extraordinary ability to perform rapid calculations in mathematics. After a
(5) problem was written on a blackboard placed in front of him, he promptly counted out the answer by tapping the low numbers with his right forefoot and multiples of ten with his left. Trickery was
(10) ruled out because Hans's owner, unlike other owners of other performing animals, did not profit financially—and Hans even performed his feats whether or not the owner was present. The psychologist
(15) O. Pfungst witnessed one of these performances and became convinced that there had to be a more logical explanation than the uncanny intelligence of a horse.

Because Hans performed only in the
(20) presence of an audience that could see the blackboard and therefore knew the correct answer, Pfungst reasoned that the secret lay in observation of the audience rather than the horse. He finally
(25) discovered that as soon as the problem was written on the blackboard, the audience bent forward very slightly in anticipation to watch Hans's forefeet. As slight as that movement was, Hans
(30) perceived it and took it as his signal to begin tapping. As his taps approached the correct number, the audience became tense with excitement and made almost imperceptible movements of the head
(35) which signaled Hans to stop counting. The audience, simply by expecting Hans to stop when the correct number was reached, had actually told the animal when to stop. Pfungst clearly demonstrated
(40) that Hans's intelligence was nothing but a mechanical response to his audience, which unwittingly communicated the answer by its body language.

Peter Farb, *Word Play: What Happens When People Talk*

5. Why was Hans's performance considered amazing by his audience?

   (1) Horses usually can't do math problems.
   (2) Hans was faster than the average horse.
   (3) Hans's owner didn't make a profit.
   (4) Hans obviously enjoyed his unusual work.
   (5) The audience couldn't figure out the trick involved.

6. Which of the following statements is the most important about what Pfungst concluded regarding Hans's performance?

   (1) Hans wasn't really a math genius.
   (2) The performance had to be in front of an audience.
   (3) The audience already knew the answer.
   (4) Hans's response was mechanical.
   (5) Body language can communicate expectations.

7. In which setting would Hans have been unable to perform his act?

   (1) in a theater
   (2) before a TV studio audience
   (3) at a small party
   (4) on the radio
   (5) at the White House

8. Why does the author use the words "logical" (line 17) and "reasoned" (line 22) in connection with psychologist Pfungst?

   (1) to make him seem more intelligent than the audience
   (2) to emphasize the scientific validity of the discovery
   (3) because they contrast with body language
   (4) because they are the basis of spoken language
   (5) to explain why Pfungst wanted to understand the secret

WHY IS ROBERT SO PUZZLED?

One summer day, my son Robert, then five years old, took me by the hand and asked me to go outside with him.

(5) Holding on tightly, he carefully walked around the house with me, looking at doors and windows and shaking his head. There was something he didn't understand.

"Mommy," he finally asked, pressing my hand with his warm, chubby fingers, "is our

(10) home broken?"

His words shot through my body, altering every protective instinct, activating my private defense system, the one I hold in reserve to ward off attacks against women

(15) and children.

"Oh, Robbie," I answered, hugging him, "did someone tell you that we have a broken home?"

"Yes," he said sweetly. "But it doesn't

(20) *look* broken!"

"It's not," I assured him. "Our house is not broken and neither are we."

I explained that "broken" is some people's way of describing a home with

(25) only one parent, usually the mother. Sometimes there was only one parent because of divorce, like us. "There are still lots of homes like ours. And they're still homes."

(30) Robbie looked relieved and went to play with his friends. I stood there, shaking with anger.

What a way to put down a little kid and me, too, I thought. I supported my

(35) three children, fed and clothed them. I was there for them emotionally and physically. I managed to keep up payments on the house. Although we struggled financially, we were happy and loving. What was

(40) "broken" about us?

Carol Kleiman, "My Home Is Not Broken, It Works"

9. When Robert asks if his home is broken, to what is he referring?
   (1) his house
   (2) his mother and father
   (3) his mother and himself
   (4) women and children
   (5) his divorced mother

10. According to this excerpt, which of the following is the best meaning for the phrase "to ward off" (line 14)?
    (1) to run away from
    (2) to object to
    (3) to defend against
    (4) to put a curse on
    (5) to accept

11. Which of the following pairs of words would best describe an important contrast between Robert and his mother as demonstrated in the passage?
    (1) whole and broken
    (2) innocent and experienced
    (3) sad and productive
    (4) angry and supportive
    (5) relieved and loving

12. Which of the following best summarizes the main idea of this excerpt?
    (1) Children are curious.
    (2) A carelessly spoken word can cause harm.
    (3) Children can recover quickly from hurt.
    (4) Adults can become angry over unimportant issues.
    (5) Divorce makes a person overly sensitive.

WHY IS SNOWBIRD MEMORABLE?

Snowbird (he never uses any other name; everyone in his world knows who he is) came to town reluctantly that winter. His wife was ill. Physically, he stood about
(5) five feet tall in his caribou-skin boots. His hands were dark and wide, the skin thick like leather, showing, as I remember my grandfather's hands had shown, the collected strength and scars of many
(10) years in the open. Snowbird's face, heavily lined, was free of expression as it peered from under the peak of a battered baseball cap. It was a sport he had never heard of. But the old eyes, even behind bifocals,
(15) were sharp and clear. Snowbird has lived in the Canadian bush, in cabins, behind lean-tos, on mattresses of boughs, and under buffalo robe blankets and the crisp stars ever since Theodore Roosevelt was
(20) President of the United States. Snowbird is unable to read words on paper. But he can read tracks and blood in the snow and branches broken certain ways, and sounds in the air. He knows the colors of
(25) good clouds and bad clouds and the sunsets and different winds that presage tomorrow's weather. He knows tales as timeless as their morals. He has some theories on modern problems. And he can
(30) speak four languages—Cree, English, Chipewyan, and dog—sometimes in the same sentence. "I'm seventy-seven years old," he told us. "I'm just beginning to grow."

Andrew H. Malcolm, *The Canadians*

13. How can Snowbird's life before he came to the town be best described?

    (1) tragic
    (2) rough
    (3) carefree
    (4) stressful
    (5) uneventful

14. Which of the following best describes how the author feels about Snowbird?

    (1) awed
    (2) fascinated
    (3) pitying
    (4) confused
    (5) sad

15. Although Snowbird cannot "read words on paper" (line 21), he is able to do which of the following?

    (1) read the feelings in a person's heart
    (2) read old tales
    (3) read the sights and sounds of nature
    (4) remember Theodore Roosevelt
    (5) teach four languages

16. Why does the author conclude this paragraph with a quotation from Snowbird himself?

    (1) to prove that he did know Snowbird
    (2) as evidence of Snowbird's age
    (3) as an example of Snowbird's knowledge of languages
    (4) to sum up Snowbird's worldview
    (5) as evidence of Snowbird's knowledge of nature

17. According to the excerpt, which of the following describes Snowbird?

    (1) young
    (2) tall
    (3) short
    (4) pale
    (5) fat

18. Which of the following best summarizes Snowbird's attitude toward his life?

    (1) He is eager to continue living and learning.
    (2) He feels he has learned all he needs to know.
    (3) He has become bored with life.
    (4) He thinks he is too old to go on.
    (5) He just wants to take it easy.

HOW IMPORTANT IS THIS GAME?

Roberto had a tremendous amount of spirit. A few years later, when he was already established in the major leagues, I get a call from the prison in Rio Piedras,
(5) inviting me to bring a softball team to play against the inmates. They knew I was a close friend of Roberto's, and since it was the off-season they asked if he could come to play with our team. I said to Roberto,
(10) *"Caramba*, they want a softball team to go to the prison to entertain the inmates. Can you come with us on Saturday?"
"Of course. Come pick me up."
At 8:30 in the morning on Saturday I
(15) go to his house and he's wearing his Pittsburgh Pirate uniform! As if he were going to a big league game! We went to the prison and everyone was very happy. I was the pitcher for our team—I was slow,
(20) and the inmates had a pretty tough bunch. In the first inning they got about five runs off me, I couldn't get a man out! Roberto, who was playing shortstop, comes to the mound and says, *"Que pasa*?" "They're
(25) hitting me," I tell him.
"Give me the ball. I don't even like to lose a game in jail," he says.
"But I'm the manager, you can't take me out."
(30) *"Out,"* he says firmly.
He had terrific speed and struck them out one after another. In the fifth inning we were catching up, but we were still a couple runs behind. He came to bat, with
(35) two men on base, and I was coaching at third base. He smacks one to right-center field and the ball really takes off. I'm waving the people home and he comes rounding second base. I signal for him to
(40) stop but he slides head first into third, and the third baseman goes flying. What a cloud of dust! He gets up, wiping himself off, and I say, "You're *loco*, an expensive big leaguer like you, sliding head first, and
(45) look at that poor prisoner over there, he still hasn't gotten up."
"I've always told you I play to win," he says. He was very proud when we won that game.

Kal Wagenheim, *Clemente!*

19. Which of the following best summarizes the main idea of this excerpt?
  (1) Roberto Clemente was a great baseball player.
  (2) Roberto Clemente loved the game of baseball.
  (3) Roberto Clemente always played to win.
  (4) Roberto Clemente enjoyed playing softball.
  (5) Roberto Clemente played prison inmates in softball.

20. Which of the following best describes how well the author knew Clemente?
  (1) He knew Clemente slightly.
  (2) He was a close friend of Clemente.
  (3) He didn't know Clemente at all.
  (4) He was one of Clemente's fans.
  (5) He was Clemente's brother.

21. Which of the following best explains Clemente's wearing his Pittsburgh Pirate's uniform to the softball game?
  (1) He wanted to show off.
  (2) He didn't know it wasn't a regular game.
  (3) He didn't have anything else to wear.
  (4) He took the game seriously.
  (5) He thought it would intimidate the inmates.

22. Based on the excerpt, what word best describes Roberto Clemente?
  (1) intense
  (2) quick-tempered
  (3) selfish
  (4) lazy
  (5) friendly

Questions 1 through 5 refer to the following review of a CD-ROM.

WHAT CAN YOU LEARN ABOUT DOGS?

Features

- Great advice and facts about everything from house training to dog shows
(5) - A bone-shape toolbar is your navigational palette

A good place to go for basic breed information if you've decided to get a dog.

There's more to a dog than just a cute
(10) face. If you've decided to get a dog and want to learn more about all the breeds out there, Inroads Interactive's CD-ROM, Multimedia Dogs 2.0, is a good place to turn.
(15) A bone-shaped toolbar is your navigational palette, and it includes brief breed narratives, informational videos, games, and other tidbits. For each type of dog you'll find a picture, a short historical
(20) write-up, and the breed characteristics. However, the write-ups don't cover temperament and weight—two important factors in choosing your dog. You must fill out a Fetch profile of the characteristics
(25) you'd welcome in a dog, and Multimedia Dogs provides a list of suitable breeds.
The most useful information in Multimedia Dogs is not in the breed anecdotes or videos, but under the Topics
(30) option. There you'll find great advice and facts about everything from house training to dog shows.
Multimedia Dogs is a good place to start if you're trying to narrow down a
(35) breed search to a few select dogs. To get more detailed facts, you're better off visiting a dog-oriented Web site or your local bookstore. If you're already a dog owner, you'll enjoy learning about other
(40) breeds and playing the Name That Dog breed-identifying game included on the CD.

Kyla K. Carlson, "Multimedia Dogs 2.0"

1. To find information about house training, which option would you choose?
   (1) Videos
   (2) Topics
   (3) Fetch
   (4) Games
   (5) Breeds

2. Why is the toolbar in this program "bone-shaped" (line 15)?
   (1) All toolbars are this shape.
   (2) The shape suggests the subject.
   (3) It is the most convenient shape.
   (4) The shape will attract dogs.
   (5) The shape will deter cat-lovers.

3. What does the reviewer consider to be a deficit in the entries for each breed?
   (1) You find too much detailed information.
   (2) You can't find out if a dog is good-natured.
   (3) You can't find out if a dog has floppy ears.
   (4) You can't find out about where the breed originated.
   (5) You can't find out what the breed looks like.

4. What can you conclude about a "Fetch profile" from the information in lines 23–26?
   It is a
   (1) list
   (2) topic
   (3) search tool
   (4) book
   (5) button

5. According to the review, how does a user navigate within the program?
   By means of
   (1) videos
   (2) a toolbar
   (3) a game
   (4) narratives
   (5) a Fetch profile

WHAT DISTINGUISHED THIS PAINTER'S WORK?

Peter Paul Rubens, Raphael and others produced magnificent paintings of biblical events showing saints, cherubs, and surprisingly, distinguished contemporaries.

(5) It was not uncommon to include among the crowd or even as principal worshipers patrons and the court in their very best finery, even a suit of armour.

The settings, too, might be the cathedral
(10) in town or a Lombardy landscape with shepherds joined by Crusaders and ruling dukes.

How Rubens included contemporary portraits in his biblical and allegorical
(15) paintings was illustrated by Christopher J. White, who lectured in Muncie earlier this month.

The distinguished art historian, director of the Ashmolean Museum at Oxford
(20) University, delivered the second annual Edmund F. Petty Memorial Lecture at the Ball State University Art Gallery.

Author of several books, including *Peter Paul Rubens: Man and Artist*,
(25) White's topic focused on Rubens and the Art of Portraiture.

"Although Rubens was not primarily a portrait painter, he did many fine ones and extended portraiture into his other works,"
(30) White pointed out.

His altarpieces and paintings of heroic scope are enlivened with the "intense vitality of people you'd recognize, meet and speak with."

(35) Rubens mixed allegory and real life. A superb altarpiece includes the portrait of an archduchess, who, though for years she had worn mourning, was painted wearing an extravagant ermine robe over
(40) a luxurious satin gown accented with four long strands of 12 millimeter pearls. She kneels on the steps of the local church with great billowing curtains overhead.

But more than trappings, the
(45) archduchess's character is defined in her face. She appears as a real person. Rubens humanized his subjects, who were often his patrons, including them in altarpieces and other major works.

(50) For such was the custom of his day. Dukes, kings, and duchesses wanted to be witnesses to the nativity scene or the raising of the cross, for instance.

With a cloud of cherubs swirling
(55) overhead, the king and queen pay homage to the heavenly host.

Rubens's strong, character-defining portraits within paintings of momentous events distinguish his work.

(60) "Portraits are his commentary on people he met as an artist and diplomat. They are quite unique for the period [17th century]," White said.

Nancy Millard, "Historian Sheds Light on Rubens and Art of Portraiture"

6. This reviewer is discussing a lecture given by whom?

   (1) a painter named Rubens
   (2) a Ball State University professor
   (3) Edmund F. Petty
   (4) a biblical illustrator
   (5) an authority on Rubens

7. Why was the portrait of the archduchess included in the lecture?

   (1) because she seemed so real
   (2) as an example of how Rubens included contemporary portraits in his paintings
   (3) as a commentary on Rubens's friendships
   (4) to illustrate how important royal patrons were to seventeenth century artists
   (5) because it is the reviewer's favorite

8. If Rubens were a modern artist, which of the following might you expect to find in his paintings?

   (1) kings in full armor
   (2) a food vendor and a senator
   (3) a cathedral and a landscape
   (4) a cloud of cherubs and saints
   (5) a self-portrait

9. How does the reviewer prepare the reader for understanding White's final comment?

   By suggesting that

   (1) including patrons was unusual
   (2) Rubens conveyed people's humanity
   (3) portraits were the custom
   (4) artists often included patrons
   (5) Rubens was a painter of allegory

CAN YOU FIND STARS IN YOUR COMPUTER?

To some, the word "RedShift" might suggest personnel transfers within the Communist Party.

(5) But to others, it's "an increase in wavelength (funny-looking letter) of electromagnetic radiation between its emission and its reception. It is quantified in terms of the wavelength change (triangle and funny-looking letter) by the

(10) relationship z equals (triangle, funny-looking letter-slash-funny-looking letter)."

They would also be the people who got their hands on a copy of "RedShift 4," an awesome planetarium-in-a-box for

(15) PCs. It's from Maris Multimedia in the United Kingdom and is published in the United States by Cinegram Media of Summit, N. J.

"RedShift 4" is the latest in a series of

(20) astronomical multimedia products and it's a way to tour the universe without having NASA's budget and toys. There are wonderful photographs of planets, galaxies and other celestial stuff, interesting

(25) multimedia lectures and a dictionary (which provided the definition above).

The curious can view the universe as far back as 4713 B.C. and as far ahead as 9999. And you can change your point of

(30) view according to celestial object and whether you are looking from the object's surface or from space above it.

Some of this stuff is well beyond those whose knowledge of astronomy is pretty

(35) much summed up in "Twinkle, Twinkle, Little Star," but there's plenty for the amateur who just wants to take a look and isn't going to follow the dancing math symbols.

(40) The user interface takes a bit of getting used to, operating mostly—but not always—like a Web browser, but the first run begins with a multimedia tutorial that more than adequately gets you started.

(45) The package contains two CD-ROMS and puts at least 80 MB and up to 300 MB onto your hard drive. Much of it is in photos, which are printable, as are the star maps. It also cross-references star

(50) catalogs.

There's a section of what amounts to heavenly trivia, which allows you to drop into cocktail party conversations tidbits such as "Seven is the maximum number

(55) of lunar and solar eclipses possible in any calendar year." And, lest anyone get his hopes up, it most recently occurred in 1917 and won't happen again until 2094.

The minimum system requirements are

(60) Windows (95, 98, 2000, ME, or NT4), 64 MB or RAB, 16-bit high-color 800-by-600 display, quad-speed CD-ROM drive and at least 2 MB of video RAM. The recommended system is at least a Pentium II at 350 MHz

(65) with 128 MB of system RAM and 16 MB of video RAM.

Installation was professional and predictable, and the uninstall program—dear to a user's heart—did what it ought to do.

(70) "RedShift 4" is available at the company's Web site for $59.95. You might find a better deal at online retailers and in stores.

An earlier version, "RedShift 3," is also available for Macs.

Larry Blasko, "'RedShift 4' Software Praised"

10. In line 5, to what does the phrase "funny-looking letter" probably refer?

A scientific

(1) problem
(2) definition
(3) symbol
(4) diagram
(5) hypothesis

11. Which of the following words best describes the overall style of the review?

(1) casual
(2) scientific
(3) academic
(4) simple
(5) serious

12. Which of the following can you conclude about the reviewer?

He

(1) thinks the software is too hard to use
(2) is an astronomer
(3) likes the software
(4) doesn't like computers
(5) thinks astronomy is boring

Questions 13 through 16 refer to the following excerpt from a movie review.

WHY IS "STAR WARS" STILL POPULAR?

To see "Star Wars" again after 20 years is to revisit a place in the mind. George Lucas' space epic has colonized our imaginations, and it is hard to stand
(5) back and see it simply as a motion picture because it has so completely become part of our memories. It's as goofy as a children's tale, as shallow as an old Saturday afternoon serial, as corny as
(10) Kansas in August—and a masterpiece. Those who analyze its philosophy do so, I imagine, with a smile in their minds. May the Force be with them….

"Star Wars" combined a new
(15) generation of special effects with the high-energy action picture; it linked space opera and soap opera, fairy tales and legend, and packaged them as a wild visual ride.
(20) "Star Wars" effectively brought to an end the golden era of early-1970s personal filmmaking and focused the industry on big-budget special effects blockbusters, blasting off a trend we are
(25) still living through. But you can't blame it for what it did; you can only observe how well it did it. In one way or another all the big studios have been trying to make another "Star Wars" ever since (pictures
(30) like "Raiders of the Lost Ark," "Jurassic Park," and "Independence Day" are its heirs). It located Hollywood's center of gravity at the intellectual and emotional level of a bright teenager.
(35) It's possible, however, that as we grow older, we retain within the tastes of our earlier selves. How else to explain how much fun "Star Wars" is, even for those who think they don't care for science
(40) fiction? It's a good-hearted film in every single frame, and shining through is the gift of a man who knew how to link state-of-the-art technology with a deceptively simple, really very powerful, story.

Roger Ebert, "Star Wars: Breakthrough Film Still Has the Force"

13. According to the author, what audience was probably targeted by "Star Wars"?
    (1) bright teenagers
    (2) movie critics
    (3) children
    (4) senior citizens
    (5) soap-opera lovers

14. Why do those who analyze "Star Wars" have a "smile in their minds" (line 12)?
    (1) They think the movie is a comedy.
    (2) They are confused by the movie.
    (3) They are amused at themselves for taking the film seriously.
    (4) They think the movie ruined Hollywood.
    (5) They usually dislike science fiction.

15. "Star Wars" spawned two successful sequels: "The Empire Strikes Back" and "Return of the Jedi." To what would this reviewer probably have attributed the success of the sequels?
    (1) gullible audiences
    (2) a successful formula
    (3) on-screen violence
    (4) a lot of luck
    (5) changing tastes

16. Which of the following best expresses the reviewer's overall opinion of the movie?
    (1) It is a flawed, expensive soap opera.
    (2) It is a special-effects movie with no central story line.
    (3) It is a brilliant special-effects movie with a powerful story.
    (4) It doesn't hold up on second viewing.
    (5) Its action can't be analyzed.

WHERE HAVE ALL THE COWBOYS GONE?

You don't have to be old to feel out of sync with your day, to yearn for a time when houses had porches and men wore hats and seldom was heard a
(5) discouraging word. There are millions of young people who feel as if they were born decades too late. And they should be able to hook right into Matt Damon's dilemma in "All the Pretty Horses."

(10) Damon plays John Grady Cole, a scion of generations of Texas ranchers, who realizes he is already an anachronism in 1949, when his parents divorce and the family spread is sold off to oil interests.
(15) It's an end-of-an-era scenario worthy of Chekhov: Indeed, it would be fitting if John's mother (who "wants to be in the live thee-ay-ter") wound up in some San Antonio community production of "The
(20) Cherry Orchard."

Determined to live out the cowboy's life as his granddaddy knew it, Cole sets out on horseback for Mexico with his buddy Rawlins (Henry Thomas) in search
(25) of unspoiled open spaces and some honest work. Their idealistic intentions are challenged when they are joined by an impulsive teenager (Lucas Black) who implicates them in a horse theft before
(30) they are barely over the Rio Grande border.

So begins Billy Bob Thornton's visually bountiful and lushly plotted screen adaptation of Cormac McCarthy's
(35) novel, which follows the two friends as they find employment with a wealthy Mexican rancher (Rubén Blades). Ted Tally's screenplay gets the off-the-cuff poetry and shuffling cowpoke-speak of
(40) McCarthy's protagonist, who unwisely pursues a clandestine romance with his employer's beautiful daughter, Maria, played by international traffic-stopper, Penelope Cruz.

(45) Thornton is a first-rate storyteller who knows how to key up our anxieties over things about to spill ("One False Move" and the upcoming "Gift"). We sense he identifies with Cole, whose easy heart gets

(50) him and his friend into trouble more than once. In contrast to his languorous directing debut, "Sling Blade," Thornton seems almost too eager to move things along here.

(55) McCarthy's winding tale contains enough turbulence to power three movies—the second half kicks into a "Shawshank Redemption" gear—and the result can feel crowded and choppy at times.

(60) But the film's swift, page-turning gait carries us with it, and it's nice to see Matt Damon in confident form after the ill-fitting demands of "The Talented Mr. Ripley." It's also refreshing to see him play off someone
(65) besides the overhyped Mr. Affleck. Henry Thomas gives an admirable performance. The former "E.T." kid has grown into a handsome critter; he wears the petulant mask well and doesn't hog the camera. But
(70) we could have lived without the coda in which kindly judge Bruce Dern offers succor to the dispirited Damon. It smacks of a therapy session, leaving us with the unfortunate final impression that Freud is
(75) to blame for the end of cowboy days.

Jan Stuart, "Horse Opera is "Pretty" Powerful"

17. How would the reviewer rate Bruce Dern's performance?
(1) poor
(2) mediocre
(3) indifferent
(4) superb
(5) cannot be determined

18. According to the reviewer, which of the following describes the pace of the movie?
(1) just right
(2) a bit too fast
(3) languorous
(4) much too fast
(5) too slow

19. According to the reviewer, what should have been left out of the film?
(1) the last scene
(2) the poetry
(3) the plot
(4) the romance
(5) the former "E.T." kid

Directions: Choose the <u>one best answer</u> to each question.

<u>Questions 1 and 2</u> refer to the following insurance policy letter.

WHAT DOES THIS INSURANCE LETTER EXPLAIN?

Dear Policyholder:

We are pleased to enclose your renewal policy. Below we have provided a quick reference of some features of your policy.

(5) We encourage you to read your policy and endorsements for a full explanation of your coverages.

Your policy premium reflects the following credit(s):

(10) PROTECTIVE DEVICE(S) CREDIT: Your home is equipped with protective devices such as smoke detectors, dead bolt locks, a burglar or fire alarm system.

Following is a brief description of some of
(15) the additional coverages (endorsements) you have chosen:

CONTENTS REPLACEMENT COST COVERAGE: If you have a loss that involves personal property, you will be
(20) paid based on the replacement cost (with no deduction for depreciation), subject to your policy limits and deductible. This coverage does not extend to certain items such as jewelry and furs.

(25) OFF PREMISES THEFT COVERAGE: This policy extends coverage for theft of personal property away from home, including theft of property in a motor vehicle, trailer, or watercraft.

(30) LOSS ASSESSMENT COVERAGE (SPECIAL COVERAGE): You have chosen to expand your coverage for additional causes of losses assessed during the policy period by your

(35) association of property owners. Please note that this policy does NOT include flood insurance. For more information, or to obtain flood insurance, please contact your insurance representative.

(40) The purpose of this letter is to provide you with an informative overview and does not replace your policy in any way. The full policy, along with operative endorsements, riders, and requirements,
(45) is enclosed. If you have any questions about your homeowners policy, please contact Finefellows Insurers at 1-800-555-1234.

Sincerely,

(50) Aaron Ables
Insurance Counselor

1. What is the purpose of this letter?
   (1) to sell more insurance coverage
   (2) to summarize the policy coverages
   (3) to serve as a legal document in place of the policy
   (4) to encourage questions from the policyholder
   (5) to help the policy owner decide on new coverages

2. If you lost property because of a flood, what reimbursement could you expect?
   (1) the full replacement cost
   (2) replacement cost with deduction for depreciation
   (3) coverage for all property except jewelry and furs
   (4) no reimbursement
   (5) the full replacement cost less your deductible

Questions 3 through 5 refer to the following memorandum.

WHAT SHOULD ERIKA DO?

MEMORANDUM

(5)
Date: 01/01/01
To: Erika Weiner, Manager of ITS
From: Ralph Burgess, Web Design
           Manager
Subject: Web Page Expansion

Dan Scoffield has asked me to supervise the expansion of our Web site. We (10) anticipate adding pages that will link a new customer-oriented inventory indexing system to the existing site index.

Staffing

The expansion will require additional staff. (15) I'll be hiring at least two freelance writers and three freelance graphic artists to work full time in-house for the duration of the project.

In addition, we'll need you to prepare a (20) team of HTML writers and Web site technicians to work with the Expansion Team. If it's necessary to hire outside consultants, contact Dan. I think he'll be supportive.

(25) ### Schedule

Here's the tentative schedule:

Week 1: Needs assessment and planning (including analysis of the current Web marketing efforts). Your team might be (30) needed for consultation, but would not be expected to participate full time.

Week 2: Copy and design development. Your team will review copy and design as needed. Your team will make technical (35) decisions in terms of programming.

Week 3: All copy and design to ITS for production and implementation. We'd need field-testing done by the end of week three, also.

(40) Let me know if this schedule seems possible. Also, let me know who will be selected as your ITS team, so that I can add the names to my Expansion Team list.

3. What is the main purpose of this memorandum?

   (1) to begin work on the graphic design phase of the project
   (2) to give feedback to the HTML writers
   (3) to help Dan in hiring decisions
   (4) to start setting up teams and scheduling
   (5) to begin the needs assessment

4. Which of the following best describes the style of the memorandum?

   (1) tedious and picky
   (2) straightforward and matter-of-fact
   (3) defensive and strained
   (4) amusing and informal
   (5) highly technical and dry

5. In an earlier memorandum to managers, Dan Scoffield (the company president) discouraged hiring outside consultants unless absolutely necessary. What message is Ralph sending Erika in lines 22–24?

   (1) Her request for outside consultants will probably be denied.
   (2) She should hire outside consultants without consulting Dan.
   (3) Only Ralph can hire outside consultants.
   (4) Outside consultants cost too much.
   (5) Dan will consider hiring consultants a necessary expense in this case.

Questions 6 through 8 refer to the following information insert.

HOW SHOULD YOU SAFEGUARD YOUR CAR TITLE?

IMPORTANT

This is your title. It is the only proof that you own this vehicle or boat. *Keep it safe.* Do *not* keep it in your vehicle or boat.

(5) This title is needed when you trade, sell, or transfer the vehicle or boat to a new owner.

Do *not* sign the title now. Complete the reverse of the title and sign it only when (10) you trade, sell, or transfer the vehicle or boat to a new owner.

Do the title and registration information match? Are both correct?

1. If the title and registration information
(15) do not match and the *registration information* is incorrect, return both documents to the Motor Vehicle Bureau.
2. If the title and registration information match but *both are incorrect,* return both
(20) documents to the Motor Vehicle Bureau.
3. If the title and registration information do not match and the *title information only* is incorrect, return this document to the Title Office for correction. You need not
(25) correct an address error on the title. DO NOT MAKE ANY CHANGE OR ADDITION TO YOUR TITLE. ANY ALTERATION WILL VOID THIS DOCUMENT.

(30) IF YOUR TITLE IS MISPLACED OR DESTROYED:

1. Apply for a duplicate with form 8602, available at the Motor Vehicle Bureau.
2. Keep your Duplicate title safe. It
(35) becomes your Current title.
3. If you find the original title, return the original (NOT the duplicate) to the Title Office of the Motor Vehicle Bureau.

(40) Further information about your Title and State Law is available in the pamphlet *Questions and Answers About Your Title,* available at the Motor Vehicle Bureau.

Director of Motor Vehicles

6. What should you do if your title information is incorrect and does not match your registration information?
   (1) return both to the Motor Vehicle Bureau
   (2) leave the information as is
   (3) submit a change of address form
   (4) return the title to the Title Office
   (5) return the registration and the title to the Title Office

7. What is the purpose of this insert?
   (1) to help title owners care for their title
   (2) to explain change of address
   (3) to rectify mistakes made by the Title Office
   (4) to clarify the difference between the Motor Vehicle Bureau and the Title Office
   (5) to help title owners sell their cars

8. Why is it important to keep the title safe?
   (1) If the title is lost, you will no longer own the car.
   (2) The Title Office does not have duplicate titles.
   (3) Applying for a new title is a long process.
   (4) Your title proves that you own the vehicle.
   (5) Your title is necessary to register the car.

Questions 9 through 13 refer to the following set of instructions.

HOW CAN YOU INSTALL YOUR NEW WINDOW FAN?

Windward Window Fan 2000

Window Installation Instructions

Conventional Sash Windows

1. Place the fan in the window horizontally
(5)   and lower the sash to secure the fan.
2. Withdraw the extenders packed in the ends of the panel fan to fill the window width.
Note: The fan has two 3" extenders in the
(10)   unit and one 8" extender in the carton. Combine all three extenders for wider windows.

Slider Windows

1. Place the fan in the window vertically
(15)   and close the window to hold the fan in place.
2. Add extenders to the top end of the panel as needed and adjust to fill the window height.
(20)   Note: Do not add extenders to the bottom end of the panel. The bottom of the fan should rest on the window pane.

Casement and Awning Windows

1. Place the fan in the window
(25)   horizontally.
2. Using the casement bracket (part c), secure the top brace of the fan to the horizontal window girder.
Note: Extenders are not necessary in a
(30)   casement window placement.

9. Which of the following best describes the style of this set of instructions?

(1) complex
(2) concise
(3) technical
(4) extensive
(5) wordy

10. Who is the intended audience for this set of instructions?

(1) children
(2) interior designers
(3) amateur home repairers
(4) senior citizens
(5) hardware salespeople

11. How are these instructions organized?

By

(1) comparing and contrasting information
(2) listing information in order of importance
(3) introducing a problem and offering a solution
(4) giving a sequence of steps
(5) discussing familiar items first, then moving on to unfamiliar items

12. How does installation in a conventional sash window differ from installation in a slider window?

(1) Extenders are not necessary in a sash window.
(2) The casement bracket is not necessary in a sash window.
(3) Extenders can be placed on either side in a sash window.
(4) Slider windows require longer extenders.
(5) Slider windows must be braced.

13. What is the purpose of italics and numbering in the instructions?

(1) They add information.
(2) They help readability.
(3) They might confuse the reader.
(4) They are merely decorative.
(5) All business documents include italics and numbering.

Questions 14 and 15 refer to the following warranty.

WHAT DOES YOUR WARRANTY COVER?

Zoomvision Inc. Audio and Video Products Limited Warranty

(5) Zoomvision Inc. (the warrantor) will repair this product with new or refurbished parts in the event of a defect in materials or workmanship. This repair will be free of charge in the U.S.A. or Puerto Rico as follows:

(10) For VCR, color TV, DVD products— labor and parts for one (1) year.

For compact disc players, radios, radio cassette players/recorders, microcassette recorders, receivers, tuners, amplifiers, equalizers, audio mixers—labor
(15) and parts for one (1) year.

For headphones, cartridges, microphones, adapters—labor and parts for ninety (90) days.

Carry-in or mail-in service in the U.S.A.
(20) can be obtained by contacting a Zoomvision Inc. authorized dealer or by calling toll free, 1-800-555-1122 to locate an authorized Service Center.

This warranty is extended only to the
(25) original purchaser. It covers failures due to defects in materials and workmanship which occur during normal use and does not cover normal wear to batteries.

The warranty does not cover damages
(30) which occur in shipment or failures that result from accidents, misuse, abuse, neglect, faulty installation, improper operation or maintenance, power-line surge, lightning damage, or commercial use.

(35) LIMITS AND EXCLUSIONS

There are no express warranties except as listed above.

(40) The warrantor shall not be liable for incidental or consequential damages resulting from the use of this product, including, without limitation, damage to tapes, records, or discs.

This warranty gives you specific legal rights. You may also have other rights
(45) which vary from state to state.

If a problem with any Zoomvision product develops during or after the warranty period, you may contact your dealer or a Service Center. If the problem is not
(50) handled to your satisfaction, write to the Zoomvision Customer Division at the company address above or call toll-free 1-800-555-1122.

14. Which of the following would probably be covered under the warranty?
    (1) a dead battery
    (2) a torn tape
    (3) a faulty TV speaker
    (4) deafness resulting from loud music
    (5) flood damage

15. What is the main purpose of this warranty?
    (1) to discourage claims
    (2) to provide legal guidelines for claims
    (3) to help sell products quickly
    (4) to tell customers how to contact the company
    (5) to encourage safe use of products

Before 1920

Directions: Choose the <u>one best answer</u> to each question.

Questions 1 through 4 refer to the following excerpt from a short story.

WHAT DOES THIS MAN LOVE?

In the latter part of the last century there
lived a man of science, an eminent
proficient in every branch of natural
philosophy, who not long before our story
(5) opens had made experience of a spiritual
affinity more attractive than any chemical
one. He had left his laboratory to the care
of an assistant, cleared his fine
countenance from the furnace smoke,
(10) washed the stain of acids from his fingers,
and persuaded a beautiful woman to
become his wife. In those days when the
comparatively recent discovery of
electricity and other kindred mysteries of
(15) Nature seemed to open paths into the
region of miracle, it was not unusual for
the love of science to rival the love of
woman in its depth and absorbing energy.
The higher intellect, the imagination, the
(20) spirit, and even the heart might all find
their congenial aliment in pursuits which,
as some of their ardent votaries believed,
would ascend from one step of powerful
intelligence to another, until the
(25) philosopher should lay his hand on the
secret of creative force and perhaps make
new worlds for himself. We know not
whether Aylmer possessed this degree of
faith in man's ultimate control over Nature.
(30) He had devoted himself, however, too
unreservedly to scientific studies ever to
be weaned from them by any second
passion. His love for his young wife might
prove the stronger of the two; but it could
(35) only be by intertwining itself with his love
of science, and uniting the strength of the
latter to his own.

Nathaniel Hawthorne, "The Birthmark"

1. In lines 5–6, to what do the words "spiritual
   affinity" refer?
   (1) Aylmer's work
   (2) chemical bonds
   (3) marriage
   (4) philosophy
   (5) intellectual connections

2. What is suggested about Aylmer in lines
   30–34?
   (1) He would always love science most.
   (2) He would never leave science
       completely.
   (3) He would never really love his wife.
   (4) His wife might want him to leave
       science.
   (5) He liked science more than people.

3. What might have been the goal of science
   in Aylmer's time?
   (1) to learn about the stars
   (2) to discover the mysteries of love
   (3) to be god-like
   (4) to help humanity
   (5) to discover electricity

4. On the basis of Aylmer's character as
   suggested in this excerpt, what kind of book
   would he be most likely to read?
   (1) an adventure novel
   (2) poetry
   (3) a scientific treatise
   (4) a history text
   (5) a romance

WHAT SHOULD CHILDREN BE TAUGHT?

"Now, what I want is, Facts. Teach
these boys and girls nothing but Facts.
Facts alone are wanted in life. Plant
nothing else, and root out everything
(5) else. You can only form the minds of
reasoning animals upon Facts: Nothing
else will ever be of any service to them.
This is the principle on which I bring up
my own children, and this is the principle
(10) on which I bring up these children. Stick
to Facts, sir!"

The scene was a plain, bare,
monotonous vault of a schoolroom, and
the speaker's square forefinger
(15) emphasized his observations by
underscoring every sentence with a line
on the schoolmaster's sleeve. The
emphasis was helped by the speaker's
square wall of a forehead, which had his
(20) eyebrows for its base, while his eyes found
commodious cellarage in two dark caves,
overshadowed by the wall. The emphasis
was helped by the speaker's mouth, which
was wide, thin, and hard set. The
(25) emphasis was helped by the speaker's
voice, which was inflexible, dry, and
dictatorial. The emphasis was helped by
the speaker's hair, which bristled on
the skirts of his bald head, a plantation of
(30) firs to keep the wind from its shining
surface, all covered with knobs, like the
crust of a plum pie, as if the head had
scarcely warehouse-room for the hard
facts stored inside. The speaker's
(35) obstinate carriage, square coat, square
legs, square shoulders—nay, his very
neckcloth, trained to take him by the
throat with an unaccommodating grasp,
like a stubborn fact, as it was—all helped
(40) the emphasis.

"In this life, we want nothing but Facts,
sir; nothing but Facts!"

The speaker, and the schoolmaster, and
the third grown person present, all backed a
(45) little and swept with their eyes the inclined
plane of little vessels then and there
arranged in order, ready to have imperial
gallons of facts poured into them until they
were full to the brim.

Charles Dickens, *Hard Times*

5. What do the speaker's forehead and eyes
   (lines 19–22) tell us about his character?

   (1) He is kind.
   (2) He is observant.
   (3) He is impenetrable.
   (4) He is quiet.
   (5) He listens well.

6. Later in the novel, the speaker's daughter,
   Louisa, marries a man she does not love.
   What attitude in the speaker foreshadows
   this action?

   (1) The speaker is envious of love.
   (2) The speaker emphasizes facts over any
       emotion.
   (3) The speaker pities children.
   (4) The speaker believes in marriage for
       money.
   (5) The speaker is very obstinate.

7. In lines 37–39, what does the comparison of
   the neckcloth with a "stubborn fact" tell us?

   (1) The neckcloth is tight.
   (2) The neckcloth is made of cotton.
   (3) The neckcloth is stylish.
   (4) The neckcloth seems hard.
   (5) The neckcloth is untidy.

8. Which of the following would probably be
   taught in a school run by the speaker?

   (1) art
   (2) mathematics
   (3) literature
   (4) gymnastics
   (5) music

Questions 9 and 10 refer to the following excerpt from a novel.

WHO IS THE ENEMY?

" ...look there, friend Sancho Panza, where thirty or more monstrous giants present themselves, all of whom I mean to engage in battle and slay...."

(5)   "What giants?" said Sancho Panza.

"Those...with the long arms, and some have them well-nigh two leagues long."

"Look, your worship," said Sancho; "what we see there are not giants but windmills,

(10)   and what seem to be their arms are the sails that turned by the wind make the millstone go."

"It is easy to see," replied Don Quixote, "that thou art not used to this business

(15)   of adventures; those are giants; and if thou art afraid, away with thee out of this...while I engage them in fierce and unequal combat."

Miguel de Cervantes, *Don Quixote*

9. Which of the following can you infer from this excerpt?

(1) Don Quixote has a vivid imagination.
(2) Don Quixote and Sancho Panza agree on what they are looking at.
(3) Sancho Panza is a coward.
(4) Don Quixote and Sancho Panza are not looking at the same objects.
(5) Don Quixote is afraid of the "giants."

10. Which of the following best describes how Don Quixote would probably react to being greatly outnumbered by enemies in a battle?

(1) He would be afraid of them.
(2) He would rely on Sancho Panza to explain things to him.
(3) He would be unconcerned.
(4) He would decide to retreat.
(5) He would attack if Sancho Panza were with him.

Questions 11 and 12 refer to the following excerpt from a novel.

WHY IS SCROOGE SATISFIED?

Sitting room, bed-room, lumber-room. All as they should be. Nobody under the table, nobody under the sofa; a small fire in the grate; spoon and basin ready; and

(5)   the little saucepan of gruel (Scrooge had a cold in his head) upon the hob. Nobody under the bed; nobody in the closet; nobody in his dressing gown, which was hanging up in a suspicious attitude against

(10)   the wall. Lumber-room as usual. Old fire-guard, old shoes, two fish baskets, washing-stand on three legs, and a poker.

Quite satisfied, he closed his door, and locked himself in; double-locked himself in,

(15)   which was not his custom. Thus secured against surprise, he took off his cravat; put on his dressing-gown and slippers, and his night-cap; and sat down before the fire to take his gruel.

Charles Dickens, *A Christmas Carol*

11. What does the inventory of rooms and objects suggest?

This man is

(1) worried about finding an intruder in his home
(2) making his will
(3) surprised at his own neatness
(4) unfamiliar with the place he is staying
(5) expecting an old friend

12. Which of the following would be the best title for this passage?

(1) Bad Habits
(2) City Night
(3) The Fright of His Life
(4) Double-Checking
(5) As Usual

Questions 13 through 15 refer to the following excerpt from a short story.

WHAT DOES SYLVIA FIND IN THE FOREST?

The next day the young sportsman hovered about the woods, and Sylvia kept him company, having lost her first fear of the friendly lad, who proved to be most

(5) kind and sympathetic. He told her many things about the birds and what they knew and where they lived and what they did with themselves. And he gave her a jack-knife, which she thought was as great a

(10) treasure as if she were a desert-islander. All day long he did not once make her troubled or afraid except when he brought down some unsuspecting singing creature from its bough. Sylvia would have liked

(15) him vastly better without his gun; she could not understand why he killed the very birds he seemed to like so much. But as the day waned, Sylvia still watched the young man with loving admiration. She had never

(20) seen anybody so charming and delightful; the woman's heart, asleep in the child, was vaguely thrilled by a dream of love. Some premonition of that great power stirred and swayed these young foresters

(25) who traversed the solemn woodlands with soft-footed silent care. They stopped to listen to a bird's song; they pressed forward again eagerly, parting the branches—speaking to each other rarely

(30) and in whispers; the young man going first and Sylvia following, fascinated, a few steps behind, with her gray eyes dark with excitement.

She grieved because the longed-for

(35) white heron was elusive, but she did not lead the guest, she only followed, and there was no such thing as speaking first. The sound of her own unquestioned voice would have terrified her—it was hard

(40) enough to answer yes or no when there was need of that. At last evening began

to fall, and they drove the cow home together, and Sylvia smiled with pleasure when they came to the place where she

(45) heard the whistle and was afraid only the night before.

Sara Orne Jewett, "A White Heron"

13. What is suggested about Sylvia's character in lines 21–23: "the woman's heart, asleep in the child, was vaguely thrilled by a dream of love"?

    (1) She is fearful.
    (2) She feels old.
    (3) She is on the verge of adulthood.
    (4) She thinks about love.
    (5) She is a dreamer.

14. What attitude toward nature do the young foresters share?

    (1) They both like birds.
    (2) They are against killing wildlife.
    (3) Nature frightens them.
    (4) Nature does not affect them.
    (5) They both prefer to be with nature.

15. Why are Sylvia and the young man taking care to be silent?

    (1) They are awed by the beauty of the forest.
    (2) They are searching for a white heron and don't want to startle it.
    (3) They are being pursued.
    (4) They don't want to frighten the cow.
    (5) They are angry.

WHAT IS TODAY'S LESSON?

Nat's face had brightened more and more as he listened, for, small as the list of his learning was, it cheered him immensely to feel that he had anything

(5) to fall back upon. "Yes, I can keep my temper—father's beating taught me that. And I can fiddle, though I don't know where the Bay of Biscay is," he thought, with a sense of comfort impossible to

(10) express. Then he said aloud and so earnestly that Demi heard him:

"I *do* want to learn, and I *will* try. I never went to school, but I couldn't help it, and if the fellows don't laugh at me, I guess I'll

(15) get on first rate—you and the lady are so good to me."

"They shan't laugh at you, if they do, I'll—I'll—tell them not to," cried Demi, quite forgetting where he was.

(20) The class stopped in the middle of 7 times 9, and everyone looked up to see what was going on.

Thinking that a lesson in learning to help one another was better than arithmetic just

(25) then, Mr. Bhaer told them about Nat, making such an interesting story out of it that the goodhearted lads all promised to lend him a hand and felt quite honored to be called upon to impart their stores

(30) of wisdom to the chap who fiddled so capitally. This appeal established the right feeling among them, and Nat had a few hindrances to struggle against, for everyone was glad to give him a "boost"

(35) up the ladder of learning.

Louisa May Alcott, *Little Men*

16. What was the class doing when Demi overheard Nat talking to himself?

(1) studying quietly
(2) taking a test
(3) listening to Mr. Bhaer tell a story
(4) having a lesson in learning
(5) reciting the multiplication tables

17. What does the author mean by "stores of wisdom" (lines 29–30)?

(1) what the boys have learned in school
(2) the knowledge of the ages
(3) wise sayings about shopkeeping
(4) stories about learning
(5) the best ways to cheat in school

18. Why does Nat decide he can "get on first rate" (line 15) even though he has never been to school before?

(1) because the other boys volunteer to help him
(2) because Demi says he can
(3) because he realizes he already has been able to learn something
(4) because he realizes that knowing the location of the Bay of Biscay is not important
(5) because he feels he is a natural scholar

19. As a teacher, Mr. Bhaer could best be described as

(1) inflexible
(2) indifferent
(3) scholarly
(4) lazy
(5) sympathetic

20. Which of the following details might Mr. Bhaer have included in his "lesson in learning"?

(1) that Nat knew the names of the European capitals
(2) how well Nat played the fiddle
(3) how important arithmetic is
(4) what an honor it was to have a scholar like Nat in the class
(5) how to find out where the Bay of Biscay is

21. What is the effect of the writer's use of dashes and repetition in line 18?

To

(1) confuse the reader
(2) show that Demi was carried away
(3) show that Demi has a speech impediment
(4) show Demi's reluctance to help Nat
(5) show Demi is talking down to Nat

Questions 22 through 25 refer to the following excerpt from a short story.

WHO'S THE PRISONER?

At Denver there was an influx of passengers into the coaches on the eastbound B. & M. express. In one coach there sat a very pretty young woman
(5) dressed in elegant taste and surrounded by all the luxurious comforts of an experienced traveler. Among the newcomers were two young men, one of handsome presence with a bold, frank
(10) countenance and manner; the other a ruffled, glum-faced person, heavily built and roughly dressed. The two were handcuffed together.

As they passed down the aisle of the
(15) coach the only vacant seat offered was a reversed one facing the attractive young woman. Here the linked couple seated themselves. The young woman's glance fell upon them with a distant, swift
(20) disinterest; then with a lovely smile brightening her countenance and a tender pink tingeing her rounded cheeks, she held out a little gray-gloved hand. When she spoke her voice, full, sweet, and
(25) deliberate, proclaimed that its owner was accustomed to speak and be heard.

"Well, Mr. Easton, if you will make me speak first, I suppose I must. Don't you ever recognize old friends when you meet
(30) them in the West?"

The younger man roused himself sharply at the sound of her voice, seemed to struggle with a slight embarrassment which he threw off instantly, and then
(35) clasped her fingers with his left hand.

"It's Miss Fairchild," he said, with a smile. "I'll ask you to excuse the other hand; it's otherwise engaged just at present. He slightly raised his right hand, bound at the
(40) wrist by the shining "bracelet" to the left one of his companion. The glad look in the girl's eyes slowly changed to a bewildered horror....

O. Henry, "Hearts and Hands"

22. On the basis of the excerpt, which one of the following words best describes the young woman's character?

(1) glum
(2) silly
(3) overbearing
(4) confident
(5) dependent

23. What is the purpose of the comparison in lines 8–12 of the two handcuffed men?

(1) to reveal the young woman's tastes
(2) to help us judge their characters
(3) to show us how varied people are
(4) to paint a picture
(5) to set a time frame

24. Why is Mr. Easton embarrassed?

He is

(1) confused
(2) naturally shy
(3) ashamed of his companion
(4) embarrassed by the handcuffs
(5) in love

25. Which of the following explains the phrase "a lovely smile brightening her countenance" in lines 20–21?

(1) Miss Fairchild recognizes the glum-faced man.
(2) Miss Fairchild enjoys traveling.
(3) The two men look odd together.
(4) Miss Fairchild enjoys looking pretty.
(5) Miss Fairchild likes Mr. Eaton.

Questions 26 through 28 refer to the following excerpt from a short story.

WHY DOES THIS MAN SAY NO?

It was on the third day, I think, of his being with me, and before any necessity had arisen for having his own writing examined, that, being much hurried to
(5) complete a small affair I had in hand, I abruptly called to Bartleby. In my haste and natural expectancy of instant compliance, I sat with my head bent over the original on my desk, and my right hand
(10) sideways, and somewhat nervously extended with the copy, so that, immediately upon emerging from his retreat, Bartleby might snatch it and proceed to business without the least
(15) delay.

In this very attitude did I sit when I called to him, rapidly stating what it was I wanted him to do—namely, to examine a small paper with me. Imagine my surprise,
(20) nay, my consternation, when, without moving from his privacy, Bartleby, in a singularly mild, firm voice, replied, "I would prefer not to."

I sat awhile in perfect silence, rallying
(25) my stunned faculties. Immediately it occurred to me that my ears had deceived me, or Bartleby had entirely misunderstood my meaning. I repeated my request in the clearest tone I could
(30) assume; but in quite as clear a one came the previous reply, "I would prefer not to."

"Prefer not to," echoed I, rising in high excitement, and crossing the room with a stride. "What do you mean? Are you
(35) moonstruck? I want you to help me compare this sheet, here—take it," and I thrust it towards him.

"I would prefer not to," said he.

I looked at him steadfastly. His face
(40) was leanly composed; his gray eye dimly calm. Not a wrinkle of agitation rippled him.... I stood gazing at him awhile, as he went on with his own writing, and then

I reseated myself at my desk. This is very
(45) strange, thought I. What had one best do? But my business hurried me. I concluded to forget the matter for the present, reserving it for my future leisure. So, calling Nippers from the other room, the
(50) paper was speedily examined.

Herman Melville, "Bartleby, the Scrivener"

26. Which word might <u>best</u> describe Bartleby?
    (1) exuberant
    (2) angry
    (3) pleasant
    (4) stubborn
    (5) loving

27. If Bartleby were working in today's version of his job, what would it be?
    (1) lawyer
    (2) bookseller
    (3) accountant
    (4) sergeant
    (5) word processor

28. What in the excerpt might explain the narrator's assertion earlier in the story that "no materials exist for a full and satisfactory biography of this man....Bartleby was one of those beings of whom nothing is ascertainable"?
    (1) Bartleby irritates the narrator.
    (2) Bartleby works in a boring job.
    (3) Bartleby's refusal to help is completely mystifying.
    (4) Bartleby is lazy.
    (5) Bartleby has been with the firm only three days.

Questions 29 through 33 refer to the following excerpt from a novel.

WHAT NEWS DOES THIS LETTER CONTAIN?

To Mrs. Saville, England
July 7th, 17–.

My Dear Sister,
    I write a few lines in haste, to say that I

(5) am safe, and well advanced on my voyage. This letter will reach England by a merchant-man now on its homeward voyage from Archangel; more fortunate than I, who may not see my native land,

(10) perhaps, for many years. I am, however, in good spirits: my men are bold, and apparently firm of purpose; nor do the floating sheets of ice that continually pass us, indicating the dangers of the region

(15) towards which we are advancing, appear to dismay them. We have already reached a very high latitude; but it is the height of summer, and although not so warm as in England, the southern gales, which blow

(20) us speedily towards those shores which I so ardently desire to attain, breathe a degree of renovating warmth which I had not expected.
    No incidents have hitherto befallen us,

(25) that would make a figure in a letter. One or two stiff gales, and the breaking of a mast, are accidents which experienced navigators scarcely remember to record; and I shall be well content, if nothing

(30) worse happen to us during our voyage.
    Adieu, my dear Margaret. Be assured, that for my own sake, as well as your's, I will not rashly encounter danger. I will be cool, persevering, and prudent.

(35)   Remember me to all my English friends.

Most affectionately yours,
R. W.

Mary Shelley, *Frankenstein*

29. In what direction is the letter writer sailing?
    (1) south, toward the Equator
    (2) west, toward America
    (3) north, toward the North Pole
    (4) east, toward Europe
    (5) It is impossible to tell.

30. What is meant by the phrase "that would make a figure in a letter" (line 25)?
    It means something that
    (1) would be important
    (2) would be understandable
    (3) would seem amusing
    (4) would scare his sister
    (5) he can remember

31. What is R. W.'s position on the ship?
    (1) common sailor
    (2) captain
    (3) navigator
    (4) passenger
    (5) stowaway

32. Which of the following best expresses R. W.'s character?
    (1) arrogant
    (2) bold
    (3) angry
    (4) timid
    (5) secretive

33. Besides informing his sister about events, what is R. W.'s purpose in writing to her?
    To
    (1) impress her
    (2) warn her
    (3) frighten her
    (4) give her advice
    (5) reassure her

Directions: Choose the one best answer to each question.

Questions 1 through 4 refer to the following excerpt from a short story.

WILL THIS SOLDIER PLAY FOOTBALL AGAIN?

We were all at the hospital every
afternoon, and there were different ways
of walking across the town through the
dusk to the hospital. Two of the ways were
(5) alongside canals, but they were long.
Always, though, you crossed a bridge
across a canal to enter the hospital. There
was a choice of three bridges. On one of
them a woman sold roasted chestnuts. It
(10) was warm, standing in front of her
charcoal fire, and the chestnuts were
warm afterward in your pocket. The
hospital was very old and very beautiful,
and you entered through a gate and
(15) walked across a courtyard and out a gate
on the other side. There were usually
funerals starting from the courtyard.
Beyond the old hospital were the new brick
pavilions, and there we met every
(20) afternoon and were all very polite and
interested in what was the matter, and sat
in the machines that were to make so
much difference.

The doctor came up to the machine
(25) where I was sitting and said: "What did you
like best to do before the war? Did
you practice a sport?"

I said: "Yes, football."

"Good," he said. "You will be able to
(30) play football again better than ever."

My knee did not bend and the leg
dropped straight from the knee to the
ankle without a calf, and the machine was
to bend the knee and make it move as in
(35) riding a tricycle. But it did not bend yet,
and instead the machine lurched when it
came to the bending part. The doctor said:
"That will all pass. You are a fortunate
young man. You will play football again
(40) like a champion."

Ernest Hemingway, "In Another Country"

1. What is the main effect of the doctor's
assurance that the narrator will "play football
again like a champion"?
   (1) We believe the doctor.
   (2) We feel that the doctor is deceiving
   himself and the patient.
   (3) We realize that the machine will work.
   (4) We see that the injury is not serious.
   (5) We realize that the doctor is a genius.

2. What is suggested by the narrator's
observation that "Beyond the old hospital
were the new brick pavilions" (lines 18–19)?
   (1) The old hospital is useless.
   (2) The old hospital is made of wood.
   (3) The new pavilions might have been
   added since the war.
   (4) The new pavilions are more beautiful
   than the old hospital.
   (5) The patients prefer the new pavilions.

3. Why does the narrator compare the
machine to "riding a tricycle"?
   (1) Riding a tricycle is hard.
   (2) Riding a tricycle is good practice for
   playing football.
   (3) The patient feels good in the machine.
   (4) The tricycle will cure the injury.
   (5) The machine and a tricycle move in the
   same way.

4. Ernest Hemingway served as an ambulance
driver in World War I and was himself
severely wounded. How might this fact have
helped him write the passage?
   (1) He wrote from experience.
   (2) He felt distant from the narrator.
   (3) He was angry with the doctor.
   (4) He had a good imagination.
   (5) Driving an ambulance is like riding a
   tricycle.

HOW PROUD IS THIS MAN?

Braggioni sits heaped upon the edge of a straight-backed chair much too small for him, and sings to Laura in a furry, mournful voice. Laura has begun to find
(5)   reasons for avoiding her own house until the latest possible moment, for Braggioni is there almost every night. No matter how late she is, he will be sitting there with a surly, waiting expression, pulling at his
(10) kinky yellow hair, thumbing the strings of his guitar, snarling a tune under his breath. Lupe the Indian maid meets Laura at the door, and says with a flicker of a glance towards the upper room, "He
(15) waits."

Laura wishes to lie down, she is tired of her hairpins and the feel of her long tight sleeves, but she says to him, "Have you a new song for me this evening?" If
(20) he says yes, she asks him to sing it. If he says no, she remembers his favorite one, and asks him to sing it again. Lupe brings her a cup of chocolate and a plate of rice, and Laura eats at the small table under
(25) the lamp, first inviting Braggioni, whose answer is always the same: "I have eaten, and besides, chocolate thickens the voice."

Laura says, "Sing, then," and Braggioni heaves himself into song and
(30) scratches the guitar familiarly as though it were a pet animal, and sings passionately off key, taking the high notes in a prolonged painful squeal. Laura, who haunts the markets listening to the ballad
(35) singers, and stops every day to hear the blind boy playing his reed-flute in Sixteenth of September Street, listens to Braggioni with pitiless courtesy, because she dares not smile at his miserable performance.
(40) Nobody dares to smile at him. Braggioni is cruel to everyone, with a kind of specialized insolence, but he is so vain of his talents and so sensitive to slights, it would require a cruelty and vanity greater
(45) than his own to lay a finger on the vast cureless wound of his self-esteem. It would require courage, too, for it is dangerous to offend him, and nobody has this courage.

Katherine Anne Porter, "Flowering Judas"

5. On the basis of Braggioni's character as revealed in the excerpt, which one of the following would he most likely do if Laura yawned during his performance?

(1) smile and ask what she'd like to hear
(2) ignore her and continue playing
(3) storm out of the room
(4) stop singing and wait
(5) ask her if she's tired

6. Why does Braggioni refuse to eat?

(1) He prefers to sing.
(2) He doesn't like rice.
(3) Chocolate is fattening.
(4) He is embarrassed.
(5) He loves chocolate.

7. What is the purpose of comparing Braggioni with the blind boy who plays the reed-flute (lines 35–36)?

(1) Braggioni is the better musician.
(2) We learn that Laura really appreciates beautiful music.
(3) The blind boy is a well-trained musician.
(4) Braggioni and the blind boy play the same instument.
(5) Braggioni is envious of the blind boy.

WHY DOES THIS MAN CARE SO MUCH?

It was not to be believed and I kept telling myself that, as I walked from the subway station to the high school. And at the same time I couldn't doubt it. I was
(5) scared, scared for Sonny. He became real to me again. A great block of ice got settled in my belly and kept melting there slowly all day long, while I taught my classes algebra. It was a special kind of
(10) ice. It kept melting, sending trickles of ice water all up and down my veins, but it never got less. Sometimes it hardened and seemed to expand until I felt my guts were going to come spilling out or that I
(15) was going to choke or scream. This would always be at a moment when I was remembering some specific thing Sonny had once said or done.

When he was about as old as the boys
(20) in my class his face had been bright and open, there was a lot of copper in it; and he'd had wonderfully direct brown eyes, and great gentleness and privacy. I wondered what he looked like now. He had
(25) been picked up, the evening before, in a raid on an apartment downtown, for peddling and using heroin.

James Baldwin, "Sonny's Blues"

8. Which of the following is the <u>best</u> description of the narrator?

   (1) a past friend of Sonny's
   (2) a high school student
   (3) an algebra teacher
   (4) someone Sonny had scared
   (5) Sonny's teacher

9. Which of the following <u>best</u> states the main idea of this passage?

   (1) The narrator is extremely worried about a person he had once known well.
   (2) The narrator uses a chunk of ice to relieve tension.
   (3) The news about Sonny doesn't surprise the narrator at all.
   (4) Boys often get into trouble with the law.
   (5) Drug abuse can touch and hurt many lives.

10. As suggested in this passage, which of the following does the narrator probably expect?

    He expects Sonny

    (1) to get out of jail because of his charming ways
    (2) to get in even more trouble
    (3) to have changed physically because of drug use
    (4) to be as gentle and direct as before
    (5) to appeal for help in getting a lawyer

11. Why does the author include a long description of the "special kind of ice" (line 9–10)?

    (1) because it is an effective cure for anxiety
    (2) as a vivid example of how distressed the narrator is
    (3) as a sharp contrast to heartburn
    (4) to show how the digestive system acts under stress
    (5) to suggest the narrator has used too much heroin

12. Which of the following <u>best</u> describes the narrator's feeling about Sonny?

    (1) disgust at what Sonny has become
    (2) fear of Sonny
    (3) relief that Sonny has been caught
    (4) regret for what Sonny once was like
    (5) pleasure that Sonny is no longer around

13. According to the excerpt, when did the narrator learn of Sonny's arrest?

    (1) when he met another teacher on the subway
    (2) after he got to school
    (3) while he was teaching class
    (4) while he was walking into the school building
    (5) before he got to school

Questions 14 through 17 refer to the following excerpt from a short story.

WHY CAN'T THIS WOMAN SAY SHE'S WRONG?

Besides the neutral expression that she wore when she was alone, Mrs. Freeman had two others, forward and reverse, that she used for all her human

(5) dealings. Her forward expression was steady and driving like the advance of a heavy truck. Her eyes never swerved to left or right but turned as the story turned as if they followed a yellow line down the

(10) center of it. She seldom used the other expression because it was not often necessary for her to retract a statement, but when she did, her face came to a complete stop, there was an almost

(15) imperceptible movement of her black eyes, during which they seemed to be receding, and then the observer would see that Mrs. Freeman, though she might stand there as real as several grain sacks

(20) thrown on top of each other, was no longer there in spirit. As for getting anything across to her when this was the case, Mrs. Hopewell had given it up. She might talk her head off. Mrs. Freeman

(25) could never be brought to admit herself wrong on any point. She would stand there and if she could be brought to say anything, it was something like, "Well, I wouldn't of said it was and I wouldn't of

(30) said it wasn't," or letting her gaze range over the top kitchen shelf where there was an assortment of dusty bottles, she might remark, "I see you ain't ate many of them figs you put up last summer."

Flannery O'Connor, "Good Country People"

14. What does the comparison of Mrs. Freeman to a "heavy truck" tell us about her nature?
    (1) She has a sweet nature.
    (2) She is unstoppable.
    (3) She likes to drive.
    (4) She tends to speed.
    (5) She comes from Detroit.

15. Why does Mrs. Freeman ask about the figs (lines 33–34)?
    (1) She is interested in food.
    (2) She is worried about Mrs. Hopewell's health.
    (3) She is disrespectful of Mrs. Hopewell's housekeeping.
    (4) She is changing the subject.
    (5) She hopes to be offered some figs.

16. On the basis of Mrs. Freeman's character as revealed in the excerpt, how might she act if she attended a meeting?
    (1) agree with all sides
    (2) stick to her position
    (3) listen quietly
    (4) be easily influenced
    (5) become the peacemaker

17. Which word best describes Mrs. Freeman?
    (1) happy
    (2) generous
    (3) silly
    (4) stubborn
    (5) bright

Questions 18 through 21 refer to the following excerpt from a novel.

WHY ARE THESE TWO MEN DISAGREEING?

...When the bell rang, George waited at the entrance of the "reception room" until a housemaid came through the hall on her way to answer the summons.

(5) "You needn't mind, Mary," he told her. "I'll see who it is and what they want. Probably it's only a pedlar."

"Thank you, sir, Mister George," said Mary; and returned to the rear of the house.

(10) George went slowly to the front door, and halted, regarding the misty silhouette of the caller upon the ornamental frosted glass. After a minute of waiting, this silhouette changed outline so that an arm could be

(15) distinguished—an arm outstretched toward the bell, as if the gentleman outside doubted whether or not it had sounded, and were minded to try again. But before the gesture was completed George

(20) abruptly threw open the door, and stepped squarely upon the middle of the threshold.

A slight change shadowed the face of Eugene; his look of happy anticipation gave way to something formal and polite.

(25) "How do you do, George," he said. "Mrs. Minafer expects to go driving with me, I believe—if you'll be so kind as to send her word that I'm here."

George made not the slightest movement.

(30) "No," he said.

Eugene was incredulous, even when his second glance revealed how hot of eye was the haggard young man before him. "I beg your pardon. I said—"

(35) "I heard you," said George. "You said you had an engagement with my mother, and I told you, No!"

Eugene gave him a steady look, and then he asked quietly: "What is the—the

(40) difficulty?"

George kept his own voice quiet enough, but that did not mitigate the vibrant fury of it. "My mother will have no interest in knowing that you came for her today," he said. "Or

(45) any other day!"

Eugene continued to look at him with a scrutiny in which began to gleam a profound anger, none the less powerful because it was so quiet. "I am afraid I do

(50) not understand you."

"I doubt if I could make it much plainer," George said, raising his voice slightly, "but I'll try. You're not wanted in this house, Mr. Morgan, now or at any other time. Perhaps

(55) you'll understand—this!"

And with the last word he closed the door in Eugene's face.

Booth Tarkington, *The Magnificent Ambersons*

18. What was the purpose of Eugene's visit?
    (1) He came to discuss business with George.
    (2) He came to argue with George.
    (3) He had been invited to dinner.
    (4) He came to see George's mother.
    (5) He came to take Mary to the movies.

19. What best explains why George told the housemaid it was probably only a pedlar at the door?
    (1) He honestly didn't know who was at the door.
    (2) He knew the housemaid didn't have any money for a pedlar.
    (3) He didn't want his mother to know Eugene had come.
    (4) He was trying to be helpful to the housemaid.
    (5) He thought it might be the housemaid's boyfriend, whom he would send away.

20. Based on what Eugene says and does in lines 22–40, what can be inferred about what he expected when he rang the bell?
    (1) He expected George to be rude.
    (2) He expected George's mother to answer the door.
    (3) He didn't think anyone would be home.
    (4) He thought George would answer and invite him in.
    (5) He didn't expect any fuss.

21. Which word best describes George and Eugene's language and behavior?
    (1) refined
    (2) casual
    (3) indifferent
    (4) friendly
    (5) unconventional

WHAT DOES CASS FIND AT HOME?

When Cass Edmonds and Uncle Buck ran back to the house from discovering that Tomey's Turl had run again, they heard Uncle Buddy cursing and bellowing
(5) in the kitchen, then the fox and the dogs came out of the kitchen and crossed the hall into the dog's room and they heard them run through the dog's room into his and Uncle Buck's room, then they saw
(10) them cross the hall again into Uncle Buddy's room and heard them run through Uncle Buddy's room into the kitchen again and this time it sounded like the whole kitchen chimney had come down and
(15) Uncle Buddy bellowing like a steamboat blowing, and this time the fox and the dogs and five or six sticks of firewood all came out of the kitchen together with Uncle Buddy in the middle of them hitting at
(20) everything in sight with another stick. It was a good race.

William Faulkner, "Was"

22. Which of the following statements <u>best</u> describes the situation in this passage?

(1) Uncle Buddy is having a dog race.
(2) Uncle Buddy is chasing a fox around the kitchen.
(3) Uncle Buddy is after the dogs that are chasing a fox around the house.
(4) The dogs are after Uncle Buddy who is chasing the fox.
(5) The fox is after the dogs who are chasing Uncle Buddy around the kitchen.

23. What probably happened to make it sound "like the whole kitchen chimney had come down" (lines 13–14)?

(1) Uncle Buddy had hit it with a stick.
(2) The noise of the race shook the bricks.
(3) Uncle Buddy's bellowing echoed in the chimney.
(4) The chase had led though the woodpile by the chimney.
(5) The chimney had fallen in on Uncle Buddy.

24. Uncle Buck and Uncle Buddy probably think of the dogs as which of the following?

They think the dogs are

(1) excellent fox hunters
(2) outdoor pets
(3) good watchdogs
(4) undisciplined animals
(5) part of the family

25. Which of the following techniques does the author use to emphasize the chaos of the scene?

(1) writing a short sentence at the conclusion
(2) putting all the action in one long sentence
(3) describing Uncle Buck's and Cass's reaction
(4) comparing Uncle Buddy's bellowing to a steamboat whistle
(5) having the action inside the house

26. To which of the following does the author compare Uncle Buddy's bellowing?

(1) a roaring fire
(2) a ship's horn
(3) a dog's bark
(4) a fox's howl
(5) a crashing chimney

27. William Faulkner once said, "One trouble with us American artists is that we take our art and ourselves too seriously." How does this quote help explain the tone of the extract?

(1) It shows how seriously Faulkner took his art.
(2) It explains the slapstick nature of the chase.
(3) It tells us about American history.
(4) It reveals Faulkner's dislike of critics.
(5) It explains the relationship between Cass and Uncle Buck.

WHAT DOES THE MAN
ON THE PHONE WANT?

A few minutes before ten, the phone rang. Mary hurried to quiet it. "Hello?"

The voice was a man's, wiry and faint, a country voice. It was asking a question,
(5) but she could not hear it clearly.

"Hello?" she asked again. "Will you please talk a little louder? I can't hear…. I said I can't hear you! Will you talk a little louder please? Thank you."

(10) Now, straining and impatient, she could hear, though the voice seemed still to come from a great distance.

"Is this Miz Jay Follet?"

"Yes; what is it?" (for there was a
(15) silence); "yes, this is she."

After further silence the voice said, "There's been a slight—your husband has been in a accident."

His head! she told herself.

(20) "Yes," she said in a caved-in voice. At the same moment the voice said, "A serious accident."

"Yes," Mary said more clearly.

"What I wanted to ask, is there a man
(25) in his family, some kin, could come out? We'd appreciate if you could send a man out here, right away."

"Yes; yes, there's my brother. Where should he come to?"

(30) "I'm out at Powell Station, at Brannick's Blacksmith Shop, bout twelve miles out the Ball Camp Pike."… She heard muttering, and another muttering voice. "Tell him he can't miss it. We'll keep
(35) the light on and a lantern out in the front."

"Do you have a doctor?"

"How's that again, ma'am?"

"A doctor, do you have one? Should I send a doctor?"

(40) "That's all right, ma'am. Just some man that's kin."

"He'll come right out just as fast as he can." Walter's auto, she thought. "Thank you very much for calling."

(45) "That's all right, ma'am. I sure do hate to give you bad news."

"Good-night."

"Good-bye, ma'am."

She found she was scarcely standing,
(50) she was all but hanging from the telephone. She stiffened her knees, leaned against the wall, and rang.

James Agee, *A Death in the Family*

28. What does the phrase "a accident" (line 18) tell us about the man on the phone?

    (1) He is kind.
    (2) He does not have formal education.
    (3) He is confident.
    (4) He is highly intelligent.
    (5) He is mumbling.

29. Combined with the earlier reference to time, what does the detail, "We'll keep the light on…" (lines 34–35) tell us?

    (1) There is fog.
    (2) The shop is well lit already.
    (3) The accident is not really too serious.
    (4) It is ten o'clock at night.
    (5) The shop is hard to find.

30. Why does Mrs. Follet not ask further about her husband's condition?

    She is

    (1) confident that he'll be okay
    (2) indifferent
    (3) too frightened
    (4) too shy
    (5) too busy

HOW VIVID IS THIS MEMORY?

The pass was high and wide and he jumped for it, feeling it slap flatly against his hands, as he shook his hips to throw off the halfback who was diving at him.

(5) The center floated by, his hands desperately brushing Darling's knee as Darling picked his feet up high and delicately ran over a blocker and an opposing linesman in a jumble on the

(10) ground near the scrimmage line. He had ten yards in the clear and picked up speed, breathing easily, feeling his thigh pads rising and falling against his legs, listening to the sound of cleats behind

(15) him, pulling away from them, watching the other backs heading him off toward the sideline, the whole picture, the men closing in on him, the blockers fighting for position, the ground he had to cross, all

(20) suddenly clear in his head, for the first time in his life not a meaningless confusion of men, sounds, speed. He smiled a little to himself as he ran, holding the ball lightly in front of him with his two hands, his knees

(25) pumping high, his hips twisting in the almost girlish run of a back in a broken field. The first halfback came at him and he fed him his leg, then swung at the last moment, took the shock of the

(30) man's shoulder without breaking stride, ran right through him, his cleats biting securely into the turf. There was only the safety man now, coming warily at him, his arms crooked, hand spread. Darling tucked

(35) the ball in, spurted at him, driving hard, hurling himself along, his legs pounding, knees high, all two hundred pounds bunched into controlled attack. He was sure he was going to get past the

(40) safety man. Without thought, his arms and legs working beautifully together, he headed right for the safety man, stiff-armed him, feeling blood spurt instantaneously from the man's nose onto

(45) his hand, seeing his face go awry, head turned, mouth pulled to one side. He pivoted away, keeping the arm locked, dropping the safety man as he ran easily toward the goal line, with the drumming of

(50) cleats diminishing behind him.

How long ago? It was autumn then, and the ground was getting hard because the nights were cold and leaves from the maples around the stadium blew across

(55) the practice fields in gusts of wind, and the girls were beginning to put polo coats over their sweaters when they came to watch practice in the afternoons…. Fifteen years.

Irwin Shaw, "The Eighty-Yard Run"

31. What does the phrase "Fifteen years" (lines 58–59) tell us about the football play?

(1) It happened fifteen years ago.
(2) It seemed like it took fifteen years to complete the pass.
(3) Darling was fifteen years old when it happened.
(4) The cheerleaders were fifteen years old.
(5) Darling played football for fifteen years.

32. Which word best describes this excerpt?

(1) implausible
(2) detailed
(3) cursory
(4) angry
(5) passionless

Directions: Choose the <u>one best answer</u> to each question.

<u>Questions 1 through 4</u> refer to the following excerpt from a short story.

WHAT IS THIS GIRL LEAVING BEHIND?

My mother had arranged with a stevedore to take my trunk to the jetty ahead of me. At ten o'clock on the dot. I was dressed, and we set off for the jetty.

(5) An hour after that, I would board a launch that would take me out to sea, where I then would board the ship. Starting out, as if for old time's sake and without giving it a thought, we lined up in the old way: I

(10) walking between my mother and my father. I loomed way above my father and could see the top of his head. We must have made a strange sight: a grown girl all dressed up in the middle of a morning, in

(15) the middle of the week, walking in step in the middle between her two parents, for people we didn't know stared at us. It was all of half an hour's walk from our house to the jetty, but I was passing through most

(20) of the years of my life. We passed by the house where Miss Dulcie, the seamstress that I had been apprenticed to for a time, lived, and just as I was passing by, a wave of bad feeling for her came over me,

(25) because I suddenly remembered that the months I spent with her all she had me do was sweep the floor, which was always full of threads and pins and needles, and I never seemed to sweep it clean enough to

(30) please her. Then she would send me to the store to buy buttons or thread, though I was only allowed to do this if I was given a sample of the button or thread, and then she would find fault even though they

(35) were an exact match of the samples she had given me. And all the while she said to me, "A girl like you will never learn to sew properly, you know." At the time, I don't suppose I minded it, because it was

(40) customary to treat the first year apprentice with such scorn, but now I placed on the dustheap of my life Miss Dulcie and everything that I had had to do with her.

Jamaica Kincaid, "A Walk to the Jetty"

1. Which word <u>best</u> describes Miss Dulcie?

   (1) generous
   (2) hard
   (3) even-tempered
   (4) insightful
   (5) fair

2. What does the detail "all dressed up" tell us about the girl?

   (1) She is rich.
   (2) She likes fine clothes.
   (3) Her trip is an important event.
   (4) Her parents are demanding.
   (5) Miss Dulcie gave her the clothes.

3. How did the girl react to Miss Dulcie's treatment of her?

   (1) She left immediately.
   (2) She rebelled.
   (3) She talked back.
   (4) She accepted it.
   (5) She excelled at her work.

4. On the basis of the excerpt, what might the narrator do if she met Miss Dulcie on the way to the jetty?

   (1) greet her warmly
   (2) walk on by
   (3) introduce her to her parents
   (4) explain why she felt ill-treated
   (5) offer to send Miss Dulcie a postcard

HOW DOES BERT REALLY FEEL?

When he found out that Manny was going to die, Bert didn't feel the way he knew he should, the way he knew everyone else would feel. Friends for
(5) twenty years, yet the sense of impending loss was tempered…by what? Bert was sorry for Manny, but thankful that it was Manny and not him. Where was the grief?

What Bert did feel was a sense of
(10) exhilaration, and he couldn't understand it. He tried to feel differently but could barely control his excitement; he was actually looking forward to telling everyone the news. He was already
(15) planning Manny's funeral….

Bert pictured the funeral. And a grand event it would be. He could see the twenty-four white cabs all freshly washed and shined, moving in a dignified procession
(20) behind the contrasting black funeral cars. People would stop what they were doing and look.

"They must have really respected that guy," they'd say. "He must have been a
(25) good cab driver."

Bert got choked up just thinking about it. There would be black crepe on all the aerials. He'd talk to Conklin about it. Hell, the guys would go for that, somebody had
(30) probably suggested it already. They could sell it to Conklin because it would be good advertising, Bert reasoned. But when Bert suggested it Conklin practically bust a gut.

"Do you realize how much it would cost
(35) us to do that? We'd have to pass almost a thousand calls to the opposition if we took all our cars off the road for an afternoon, and you can bet there would be a certain percentage of that business we'd never get
(40) back. Besides, Mankiewitz isn't dead yet."

"He will be."

"I don't know. I had an uncle they gave up on a couple of times. He's still living."

"Have you seen him lately?'" Bert knew
(45) the answer but he hoped he might embarrass Conklin a little. That afternoon Manny's eyes had been kind of dull and lifeless, and his two-day beard was like a skiff of snow on his face.

W. P. Kinsella, "Mankiewitz Won't Be Bowling Tuesday Nights Anymore"

5. Which of the following best describes Bert's relationship with Manny?

   (1) Bert is the funeral director for Manny's funeral.
   (2) Bert is Manny's boss.
   (3) Manny is Bert's boss.
   (4) Bert and Manny are longtime friends.
   (5) Bert is Manny's only living relative.

6. According to the excerpt, which of the following most concerned Bert?

He was concerned about Manny's

   (1) absence from work
   (2) death
   (3) funeral
   (4) layoff
   (5) visit from Conklin

7. Which new profession would best fit Bert's personality?

   (1) clergyman
   (2) physician
   (3) sympathy card writer
   (4) special events director
   (5) ad writer

CAN SHE WIN THAT RACE?

Every time, just before I take off in a
race, I always feel like I'm in a dream, the
kind of dream you have when you're sick
with fever and feel all hot and weightless. I
(5) dream I'm flying over a sandy beach in the
early morning sun, kissing the leaves of
the trees as I fly by. And there's always
the smell of apples, just like in the country
when I was little and used to think I was a
(10) choo-choo train, running through the fields
of corn and chugging up the hill to the
orchard. And all the time I'm dreaming this,
I get lighter and lighter until I'm flying over
the beach again, getting blown through
(15) the sky like a feather that weighs nothing
at all. But once I spread my fingers in
the dirt and crouch over the Get on Your
Mark, the dream goes and I am solid
again and am telling myself, Squeaky you
(20) must win, you must win, you are the
fastest thing in the world, you can even
beat your father up Amsterdam if you
really try. And then I feel my weight coming
back just behind my knees then down to
(25) my feet then into the earth and the pistol
shot explodes in my blood and I am off
and weightless again, flying past the other
runners, my arms pumping up and down
and the whole world is quiet except for the
(30) crunch as I zoom over the gravel in the
track. I glance to my left and there is no
one. To the right, a blurred Gretchen, who's
got her chin jutting out as if it would win
the race all by itself. And on the other side
(35) of the fence is Raymond with his arms
down to his side and the palms tucked up
behind him, running in his very own style,
and it's the first time I ever saw that and
I almost stop to watch my brother on his
(40) first run. But the white ribbon is bouncing
toward me and I tear past it, racing into the
distance till my feet with a mind of their
own start digging up footfuls of dirt and
brake me short. Then all the kids standing

(45) on the side pile on me, banging me on the
back and slapping my head with their May
Day programs, for I have won again and
everybody on 151st Street can walk tall for
another year.

Toni Cade Bambara, "Raymond's Run"

8. Earlier in the story, the narrator tells us, "I'd
much rather just knock you down and take
my chances even if I am a little girl with
skinny arms and a squeaky voice… If things
get too rough, I run." What does this
passage add to our understanding of the
narrator's running ability?

(1) She uses her ability to protect herself.
(2) She learned to run at school.
(3) Running is pure pleasure.
(4) She runs for a living.
(5) She only runs in track shoes.

9. How does the narrator feel as the starter's
pistol sounds?

(1) solid
(2) flighty
(3) slow
(4) weightless
(5) nervous

10. Why does the narrator think that she
"can even beat" her father in a race?
(lines 21–22)

(1) She usually beats her father.
(2) She thinks her father will cheer her on.
(3) She feels as if she can beat anyone.
(4) She feels defeated.
(5) She feels sorry for her father.

IS THE TRAIN COMING?

The three of us just sat looking across the water then. And then we heard the next northbound freight coming, and he stood up and got ready; and he said we could
(5) watch him but we better not try to follow him this time, and we promised, and we also promised to go to school the next morning.

So then we came back up the embankment, because the train was that close, and he stood looking at us, with the
(10) guitar slung across his back. Then he put his hands on our shoulders and looked straight into our eyes, and you knew you had to look straight back into his, and we
(15) also knew that we were no longer supposed to be ashamed in front of him because of what we had done. He was not going to tell. And we were not going to let him down.

Make old Luze proud of you, he said
(20) then, and he was almost pleading. *Make old Luze glad to take his hat off to you some of these days. You going further than old Luze ever dreamed of. Old Luze ain't been nowhere. Old Luze don't know*
(25) *from nothing.*

And then the train was there and we watched him snag it and then he was waving goodbye.

Albert Murray, "Train Whistle Guitar"

11. To whom does the repeated "he" in this passage refer?

    (1) the narrator
    (2) the narrator's father
    (3) part of the "we" in the last sentence (lines 26–28)
    (4) the engineer of the train
    (5) old Luze

12. The first line of the passage refers to "the three of us." Which of the following is probably two of the three?

    (1) hoboes
    (2) criminals
    (3) parents
    (4) schoolchildren
    (5) teachers

13. What is the best reason that many of the sentences in the first two paragraphs are very long?

    (1) to emphasize the suspense of waiting
    (2) because there is no dialogue
    (3) as a contrast to the first sentence
    (4) to contrast with the sentences of dialogue
    (5) because the ideas expressed are complex

14. What action is described by "snag it" (line 27)?

    (1) waving from the train
    (2) getting on the train
    (3) going up the embankment
    (4) waiting for the train
    (5) watching the train from the embankment

15. Which word best describes old Luze's feelings as they are expressed in his words?

    (1) anger
    (2) terror
    (3) concern
    (4) indifference
    (5) amusement

WHY IS THE MEMORY SO PAINFUL?

I'd done a lot of thinking about Lee in the last year, remembering him the way he was at four and five and six. Partly, I imagine, because the news of his mom got
(5) me thinking about the old days, but some because he was the only little kid I've ever been around and there'd be lots of times when I'd think, That's what our kid'd been like now. That's what our kid'd be saying
(10) now. And in some ways he was good to compare to, in some ways not. He always had a lot of savvy but never much sense; by the time he started school he knew his multiplication tables all the way to the
(15) sevens, but never was able to figure why three touchdowns comes to twenty-one points if a team kicked all their conversions, though I took him to ball games till the world looked level. I remember—let's see,
(20) I guess when he was nine or ten or so—I tried to teach him to throw jump passes. I'd run out and he'd pass. He wasn't none too bad an arm, either, and I figured he should make somebody a good little quarterback
(25) someday if he would get his butt in gear to match his brains; but after ten or fifteen minutes he'd get disgusted and say, "It's a stupid game anyway; I don't care if I ever learn to pass."

Ken Kesey, *Sometimes a Great Notion*

16. Why does the narrator think Lee didn't have "much sense" (line 12)?

   (1) because Lee couldn't learn multiplication
   (2) because Lee wasn't interested in football
   (3) because Lee was too little to have sense
   (4) because the boy would never become a good quarterback
   (5) because the boy had a lot of savvy

17. On the basis of the narrator's description, which of the following is true?

   (1) Lee's mother went to football games with Lee.
   (2) Lee was smart, but baffled by football scoring.
   (3) Lee was a great quarterback.
   (4) The narrator had been around many little kids.
   (5) The narrator and Lee hadn't been to any football games.

WHAT MAKES THIS BOY STUDY?

When school began in September, before Cohen would once again suggest giving the bird the boot, Edie prevailed on him to wait a little while until Maurie adjusted.
(5) "To deprive him right now might hurt his school work, and you know what trouble we had last year."
"So okay, but sooner or later the bird goes. That I promise you."
(10) Schwartz, though nobody had asked him, took on full responsibility for Maurie's performance in school. In return for favors granted, when he was let in for an hour or two at night, he spent most of his time
(15) overseeing the boy's lessons. He sat on top of the dresser near Maurie's desk as he laboriously wrote out his homework. Maurie was a restless type and Schwartz gently kept him to his studies. He also
(20) listened to him practice his screechy violin, taking a few minutes off now and then to rest his ears in the bathroom. And they afterwards played dominoes. The boy was an indifferent checker player and it was
(25) impossible to teach him chess. When he was sick, Schwartz read him comic books though he personally disliked them. But Maurie's work improved in school and even his violin teacher admitted his
(30) playing was better. Edie gave Schwartz credit for these improvements though the bird pooh-poohed them.

Bernard Malamud, "The Jewbird"

18. How could Schwartz be <u>best</u> described?

   (1) a well-trained pet
   (2) an unwelcome visitor
   (3) an intellectual talking bird
   (4) an indifferent tutor
   (5) an avid chess fan

19. The author probably intends the reader to see this scene as which of the following?

   (1) realistic
   (2) melodramatic
   (3) slightly fanciful
   (4) slightly mysterious
   (5) totally unbelievable

WHY IS THIS BOY'S FATHER HATED?

But it was not until many years later that I caught one fleeting, terrifying glimpse of just how hated an Interpreter could be. I was in secondary school then (5) and it was our half-term holiday. As my home village was too far away and I didn't want to spend the holiday in school I decided to go with one of my friends to his home which was four or five miles away.

(10) His parents were very happy to see us and his mother at once went to boil some yams for us.

After we had eaten, the father who had gone out to buy himself some snuff (15) came hurrying back. To my surprise he asked his son what he said my name was again.

"Odili Samalu."

"Of what town?"

(20) There was anxiety, an uneasy tension in his voice. I was afraid.

"Urua, sir," I said.

"I see," he said coldly. "Who is your father?"

(25) "Hezekiah Samalu," I said and then added quickly, "retired District Interpreter." It was better, I thought, to come out with it all at once and end the prolonged interrogation.

(30) "Then you cannot stay in my house," he said with that evenness of tone which our people expect a man of substance to use in moments of great crisis when lesser men and women would make loud, (35) empty noises.

"Why, Papa, what has he done?" asked my friend in alarm.

"I have said it…. I don't blame you, my son, or you either, because no one has (40) told you. But know it from today that no son of Hezekiah Samalu's shelters under my roof." He looked outside. "There is still light and time for you to get back to the school."

(45) I don't think I shall ever know just in what way my father had wronged that man.

Chinua Achebe, *A Man of the People*

20. Why does the narrator quickly add "retired District Interpreter" in line 26?

   (1) He is afraid his father will be confused with someone else.
   (2) He is proud of his father.
   (3) He wants to end the interrogation.
   (4) He wants to impress his friend's father.
   (5) He is trying to conceal his father's identity.

21. What word best describes Odili Samalu's behavior?

   (1) polite
   (2) arrogant
   (3) shy
   (4) silly
   (5) flippant

22. On the basis of the selection, how will Odili spend subsequent holidays?

   (1) at home
   (2) at school
   (3) at another friend's house
   (4) at the same friend's house
   (5) on a trip alone

23. Why does the friend's father accept Odili at first?

   (1) He is very suspicious, but overcomes his feelings.
   (2) His wife encourages him.
   (3) He does not recognize Odili's name.
   (4) He really likes the District Interpreter.
   (5) He does not want to punish his son.

HOW CAN AN UMBRELLA BE SO BEAUTIFUL?

The umbrella glowed like a scepter on the blue carpet while Mona, slumping over the keyboard, managed to eke out a fair rendition of a catfight. At the end of the
(5) piece, Miss Crosman asked her to stand up.

"Stay right there," she said, then came back a minute later with a towel to cover the bench. "You must be cold," she
(10) continued. "Shall I call your mother and have her bring over some dry clothes?"

"No," answered Mona. "She won't come because she…"

"She's too busy," I broke in from the
(15) back of the room.

"I see." Miss Crosman sighed and shook her head a little. "Your glasses are filthy, honey," she said to Mona. "Shall I clean them for you?"
(20) Sisterly embarrassment seized me. Why hadn't Mona wiped her lenses when I told her to? As she resumed abuse of the piano, I stared at the umbrella. I wanted to open it, twirl it around by its slender silver
(25) handle; I wanted to dangle it from my wrist on the way to school the way the other girls did. I wondered what Miss Crosman would say if I offered to bring it to Eugenie at school tomorrow. She would
(30) be impressed with my consideration for others; Eugenie would be pleased to have it back; and I would have possession of the umbrella for an entire night. I looked at it again, toying with the idea of asking for
(35) one for Christmas. I knew, however, how my mother would react.

"Things," she would say. "What's the matter with a raincoat? All you want is things, just like an American."

Gish Jen, "The White Umbrella"

24. On the basis of the narrator's description, what word best describes Mona's piano playing?
    (1) passionate
    (2) poor
    (3) impressive
    (4) turbulent
    (5) cold

25. What difference between the sisters is emphasized by the narrator's interruption in lines 14–15?
    (1) They have different talents.
    (2) They have different clothes.
    (3) The narrator is more secretive than Mona.
    (4) Mona dislikes the piano more than the narrator.
    (5) The narrator is happier than Mona.

26. To whom does the umbrella belong?
    (1) Miss Crosman
    (2) the narrator
    (3) Mona
    (4) Eugenie
    (5) the mother

27. What does the mother's anticipated reaction in lines 37–39 tell us about the family?

    They
    (1) are poor
    (2) are materialistic
    (3) are music-loving
    (4) rarely celebrate Christmas
    (5) have recently immigrated

WHAT DOES JOE KNOW?

Joe nodded and smiled a lot. "Yes ma'am. Certainly. I will look at the pictures again. The other officers, the ones in uniform, they show me the pictures, too."

(5) She stood on the customers' side of the counter. Candy had to be a big seller. There was an incredible variety, much of it costing a nickel. She hadn't seen anything like it since she was a kid. She could almost (10) taste the jawbreakers and Mary Janes.

Joe looked at the photographs of R. D., both dead girls, and a few anonymous perps currently doing time in Joliet. She had added morgue shots of Danny Jones and (15) Ruth Price and a mug shot of Glodine, one of the women associated with R. D. who had been arrested once for prostitution.

Joe identified Teresa and Carmen. He hesitated when he came to the snapshot (20) of Price. "This is the woman who was killed last night?"

"Yes."

He seemed to want to tell her something. She waited.

(25) "I have seen her."

"Was she a customer?"

Again he hesitated.

"She's dead," Marti reminded him. "What can you tell me?"

(30) "This old woman, she comes through the alley. On Thursday. Other old ones come too."

He seemed uneasy and moved to the rear of the store. He stopped at a long case (35) filled with fruit and vegetables. Everything looked fresh except for some produce stacked on an unrefrigerated shelf.

"On Thursday, what was delivered on Monday I sell at half price." He pointed to (40) the unrefrigerated produce, a little wilted but not spoiled. "What is left when I am ready to close I put out with the garbage. In a box, separate. The old ones come. They take it."

(45) "I could still sell," he said, "but I put out. In my country, there is hunger. Here there are so many rules. Is wrong, illegal that I put it out? I do not put it with the rest of the garbage, I keep it separate. The old

(50) ones know."

"It's okay," she assured him, unwilling to get involved with health-code violations.

"You can put out whatever you want and package it any way you want to." At least (55) she thought so. "There are soup kitchens, churches, and other places that give out food."

"Yes, yes. But the old ones, they come here. They do not have to beg. Is there and (60) is free and nobody to pity them. Is almost like shopping." He handed back Ruth Price's photo. "This one, she liked oranges. And sometimes a peach. They do not take more than they need. Is legal?"

(65) "It's okay," she repeated. She didn't tell him that she was glad he put the produce out, glad that Ruth Price got a few oranges every week and had eaten one last night before she died.

Eleanor Taylor Bland, *Slow Burn*

28. In this excerpt, Ruth Price is which of the following?

    (1) customer
    (2) victim
    (3) photographer
    (4) police officer
    (5) neighbor

29. Which of the following best describes what is happening in this excerpt?

    (1) Joe is trying to sell bad produce to customers.
    (2) The police want Joe to identify some people who have been killed.
    (3) The police are questioning Joe for putting food out for people to take.
    (4) Joe is trying to keep vagrants away from his store.
    (5) A photographer is trying to sell Joe some photographs.

30. Which of the following best describes Joe's behavior toward the "old ones"?

    (1) He tried to help them.
    (2) He wanted to have them arrested.
    (3) He didn't pay any attention to them.
    (4) He was afraid of them.
    (5) He wanted them to find jobs.

Questions 31 through 35 refer to the following excerpt from a short story.

WHAT HAS BUDDY LOST?

This is our last Christmas together.

Life separates us. Those who Know Best decide that I belong in a military school. And so follows a miserable succession of
(5) bugle-blowing prisons, grim reveille-ridden summer camps. I have a new home too. But it doesn't count. Home is where my friend is, and there I never go.

And there she remains, puttering around
(10) the kitchen. Alone with Queenie. Then alone. ("Buddy dear," she writes in her wild hard-to-read script, "yesterday Jim Macy's horse kicked Queenie bad. Be thankful she didn't feel much. I wrapped her in a Fine
(15) Linen sheet and rode her in the buggy down to Simpson's pasture where she can be with all her Bones....") For a few Novembers she continues to bake her fruitcakes single-handed; not as many, but
(20) some: And, of course, she always sends me "the best of the batch." Also, in every letter she encloses a dime wadded in toilet paper: "See a picture show and write me the story." But gradually in her letters
(25) she tends to confuse me with her other friend, the Buddy who died in the 1880s; more and more, thirteenths are not the only days she stays in bed: A morning arrives in November, a leafless birdless coming of
(30) winter morning, when she cannot rouse herself to exclaim: "Oh my, it's fruitcake weather!"

And when that happens, I know it. A message saying so merely confirms a piece
(35) of news some secret vein had already received, severing from me an irreplaceable part of myself, letting it loose like a kite on a broken string. That is why, walking across a school campus on this particular December
(40) morning, I keep searching the sky. As if I expected to see, rather like hearts, a lost pair of kites hurrying toward heaven.

Truman Capote, "A Christmas Memory"

31. What phrase best describes how the narrator views military school?

As

(1) solitary and quiet
(2) comfortable
(3) confining and harsh
(4) like home
(5) like camp

32. For Buddy's elderly friend, what is "fruitcake weather"?

(1) bitterly cold
(2) slightly chilly
(3) hot and humid
(4) warm and sunny
(5) rainy

33. Which of the following is true about Buddy's friend after he left home?

She

(1) was depressed
(2) found a new friend
(3) became superstitious
(4) started a bakery
(5) got a new pet

34. When Buddy's friend dies, which of the following reasons best explains why he searches the sky for a lost pair of kites?

(1) Clouds help him to relax.
(2) His hobby is flying kites.
(3) He thinks she is happy now.
(4) He needs something to do.
(5) Part of him feels lost.

35. Based on this excerpt, why do you think Buddy never goes to what he considers to be home?

(1) His family won't let him.
(2) He didn't like it there.
(3) His friend told him to leave.
(4) He prefers to stay in military school.
(5) He wants a new home.

Directions: Choose the <u>one best answer</u> to each question.

<u>Questions 1 through 4</u> refer to the following excerpt from a poem.

WHAT KIND OF PERSON WAS LUCINDA?

Lucinda Matlock

I went to the dances at Chandlerville,
And played snap-out at Winchester.
One time we changed partners,
Driving home in the moonlight of middle June,
(5)   And then I found Davis.
We were married and lived together for seventy years.
Enjoying, working, raising the twelve children,
Eight of whom we lost
Ere I had reached the age of sixty.
(10)   I spun, I wove, I kept the house, I nursed the sick,
I made the garden, and for holiday
Rambled over the fields where sang the larks,
And by Spoon River gathering many a shell,
And many a flower and medicinal weed—
(15)   Shouting to the wooded hills, singing to the green valleys.
At ninety-six I had lived enough, that is all,
And passed to a sweet repose.
What is this I hear of sorrow and weariness,
Anger, discontent and drooping hopes?
(20)   Degenerate sons and daughters,
Life is too strong for you—
It takes life to love Life.

Edgar Lee Masters, "Lucinda Matlock"

1. Which of the following <u>best</u> summarizes Lucinda Matlock's life?

   (1) She lived a long life.
   (2) She worked hard for many years.
   (3) She lived an active, happy life.
   (4) She was disappointed in her children.
   (5) She preferred pleasure to work.

2. What is the <u>best</u> explanation for who the "degenerate sons and daughters" (line 20) are?

   (1) her own children
   (2) other children in the town
   (3) previous generations
   (4) later generations
   (5) her own generation

3. What does "Shouting to the wooded hills, singing to the green valleys" (line 15) suggest about Lucinda?

   (1) She had an inner joy.
   (2) She was frivolous.
   (3) She was always glad to escape work.
   (4) She liked to be loud when she could.
   (5) She was a little odd but happy.

4. Which piece of advice would Lucinda most likely give to women today?

   (1) Do what you have to do.
   (2) Don't count on your children.
   (3) Take it easy and life will work out.
   (4) Have fun while you can.
   (5) Work hard, but enjoy life.

WHAT IS THIS GIRL DOING?
The Solitary Reaper

Behold her, single in the field,
Yon solitary Highland Lass!
Reaping and singing by herself;
Stop here, or gently pass!
(5) Alone she cuts and binds the grain,
And sings a melancholy strain;
O listen! For the vale profound
Is overflowing with the sound.

No Nightingale did ever chaunt
(10) More welcome notes to weary bands
Of travelers in some shady haunt,
Among Arabian sands;
A voice so thrilling ne'er was heard
In springtime from the Cuckoo-bird,
(15) Breaking the silence of the seas
Among the farthest Hebrides.

Will no one tell me what she sings?
Perhaps the plaintive numbers flow
For old, unhappy, far-off things,
(20) And battles long ago:
Or is it some more humble lay,
Familiar matter of today?
Some natural sorrow, loss, or pain,
That has been, and may be again?

(25) Whate'er the theme, the Maiden sang
As if her song could have no ending;
I saw her singing at her work,
And o'er the sickle bending:
I listened, motionless and still;
(30) And, as I mounted up the hill,
The music in my heart I bore,
Long after it was heard no more.

William Wordsworth, "The Solitary Reaper"

5. Which of the following statements about the highland lass's song is true?

   (1) It is sung in Arabian.
   (2) It is completely comprehensible.
   (3) It is a common tune.
   (4) It is about city life.
   (5) It is sad.

6. Which of the following best describes how the last stanza differs from the first three stanzas?

   (1) The speaker uses contractions.
   (2) The speaker uses rhyming lines.
   (3) The speaker shifts the focus to himself.
   (4) The speaker is no longer concerned with the girl and her song.
   (5) The speaker becomes unhappy about what he has seen.

7. Which of the following best summarizes the feeling expressed by the speaker in the last three lines of the poem?

   (1) He will be haunted by the song until he learns the words.
   (2) The scene was pleasing but not memorable.
   (3) This walk was a pleasant way to spend an afternoon.
   (4) This experience will remain in his memory.
   (5) He will write a song based on the singing he has heard.

WHAT IS THE NARRATOR WATCHING?

There's Been a Death
in the Opposite House

There's been a death in the
    opposite house
As lately as today.
I know it by the numb look
(5) Such houses have a way.

The neighbors rustle in and out,
The doctor drives away.
A window opens like a pod,
Abrupt, mechanically;

(10) Somebody flings a mattress out,
The children hurry by;
They wonder if it died on that,
I used to when a boy.

The minister goes stiffly in
(15) As if the house were his,
And he owned all the mourners now,
And little boys besides;

And then the milliner, and the man
Of the appalling trade,
(20) To take the measure of the house.
There'll be that dark parade

Of tassels and of coaches soon;
It's easy as a sign,
The intuition of the news
(25) In just a country town.

Emily Dickinson, "There's Been a Death in the
Opposite House"

8. Which of the following has the speaker not
   yet seen?

   (1) the neighbors
   (2) the doctor
   (3) the children
   (4) the minister
   (5) the funeral

9. With which of the following words does
   the poet emphasize the image of the "numb
   look" (line 4) of the house?

   (1) rustle
   (2) mechanically
   (3) flings
   (4) appalling
   (5) dark

10. What is being described in all but the first
    and last stanzas?

    (1) mourners of the dead person
    (2) horror of death
    (3) reactions of the speaker
    (4) activities of the living
    (5) emotional distress caused by a death

11. Why does the poet use the phrase "it died
    on that" (line 12) to explain the children's
    thoughts?

    (1) to show that the children don't use good
        grammar
    (2) to explain why the mattress was thrown
        out the window
    (3) to explain why the children hurry
    (4) to suggest that death is mysterious and
        alien to children
    (5) to make clear where the death took place

12. Which of the following describes who the
    speaker in the poem is?

    (1) daughter of the deceased
    (2) man living across the street
    (3) young neighbor boy
    (4) son of the deceased
    (5) woman living next door

13. To whom does "the man of the appalling
    trade" (lines 18–19) most likely refer?

    (1) mail carrier
    (2) gardener
    (3) minister
    (4) undertaker
    (5) doctor

Questions 14 through 17 refer to the following poem.

WILL THIS MAN EVER REST?

Is My Team Ploughing?

"Is my team ploughing,
That I was used to drive
And hear the harness jingle
When I was man alive?"

(5) Aye, the horses trample,
The harness jingles now;
No change though you lie under
The land you used to plough.

"Is football playing
(10) Along the river shore,
With lads to chase the leather,
Now I stand up no more?"

Aye, the ball is flying,
The lads play heart and soul;
(15) The goal stands up, the keeper
Stands up to keep the goal.

"Is my girl happy,
That I thought hard to leave,
And has she tired of weeping
(20) As she lies down at eve?"

Aye, she lies down lightly,
She lies not down to weep:
Your girl is well contented.
Be still, my lad, and sleep.

(25) "Is my friend hearty,
Now I am thin and pine;
And has he found to sleep in
A better bed than mine?"

Yes, lad, I lie easy,
(30) I lie as lads would choose;
I cheer a dead man's sweetheart,
Never ask me whose.

A. E. Housman, "Is My Team Ploughing?"

14. What is the purpose of the use of quotation marks?

    (1) to indicate that a man is talking to himself
    (2) to show he is quoting from another work
    (3) to suggest that there are two speakers
    (4) to suggest the speaker is directly addressing the reader
    (5) to separate quotation from description

15. Which of the following best explains the structure of this poem?

    (1) It is a simple speech.
    (2) It is an imaginary conversation.
    (3) It is a drama with many characters.
    (4) It is chaotic.
    (5) It is told in episodes.

16. Which of the following best describes the condition of the speaker who is asking questions?

    (1) He is asleep.
    (2) He has left the country.
    (3) He has lost his girlfriend.
    (4) He is happy.
    (5) He is dead.

17. Which of the following best expresses the main idea of this poem?

    (1) Friends can't be trusted with women.
    (2) A woman will quickly forget her man.
    (3) Life continues even after an individual dies.
    (4) The dead can come back from the grave to haunt the living.
    (5) Our souls will live forever.

Questions 18 through 22 refer to the following poem.

WHAT DO WE FIND IN THE SEA?

maggie and milly and molly and may

maggie and milly and molly and may
went down to the beach (to play one day)

and maggie discovered a shell that sang
so sweetly she couldn't remember her troubles, and

(5)   milly befriended a stranded star
whose rays languid fingers were;

and molly was chased by a horrible thing
which raced sideways while blowing bubbles: and

may came home with a smooth round stone
(10)   as small as a world and as large as alone.

For whatever we lose (like a you or me)
it's always ourselves we find in the sea.

e. e. cummings, "maggie and milly and molly and may"

18. According to the poem, what did the four girls do at the beach?

    (1) They went fishing.
    (2) They got lost.
    (3) They each found something.
    (4) They decided that they were good playmates.
    (5) They fell in love with the sea.

19. Which of these statements can be inferred from the poem?

    (1) maggie had no troubles.
    (2) milly had trouble making friends.
    (3) maggie and may were troubled by their discoveries.
    (4) molly was more easily scared than the others.
    (5) may had the best time.

20. Since this poet does not use capital letters in the normal ways, which of the following best explains why he capitalized "For" in line 11?

    (1) It begins a complete sentence.
    (2) It emphasizes the break between the story and the poet.
    (3) He wanted to break his own rule of capitalization.
    (4) It indicates that the rhythm of the poem is changing.
    (5) It helps to make the poem more lighthearted.

21. Why does the poet probably use the similes "as small as a world and as large as alone" (line 10)?

    (1) to describe the stone realistically
    (2) to make the stone seem heavy
    (3) to emphasize how round and smooth the stone is
    (4) to suggest the mysterious quality may saw in the stone
    (5) to compare the stone to maggie's shell

22. Which of the following best describes the effect of the girls' names all beginning with the letter m?

    (1) It implies that the girls are all alike.
    (2) It helps the reader remember the girls' names.
    (3) It gives popular girls' names.
    (4) It provides a boring quality the poet wants.
    (5) It gives the poem a pleasing repetition of sounds.

WHAT HAPPENS AS THE CHILD SLEEPS?
A Poem for Emily

Small fact and fingers and farthest one from me,
a hand's width and two generations away,
in this still present I am fifty-three.
You are not yet a full day.

(5)   When I am sixty-three, when you are ten,
and you are neither closer nor as far,
your arms will fill with what you know by then,
the arithmetic and love we do and are.

When I by blood and luck am eighty-six
(10)   and you are some place else and thirty-three
believing in sex and god and politics
with children who look not at all like me,

some time I know you will have read them this
so they will know I love them and say so
(15)   and love their mother. Child, whatever is
is always or never was. Long ago,

a day I watched a while beside your bed,
I wrote this down, a thing that might be kept
a while, to tell you what I would have said
(20)   when you were who knows what and I was dead
which is I stood and loved you while you slept.

Miller Williams, "A Poem for Emily"

23. Which of the following best characterizes the situation in this poem?

    (1) a mother speaking to her newborn daughter
    (2) a father writing to his baby son
    (3) a man speaking to his newborn grandson
    (4) a man writing to his newborn granddaughter
    (5) a man writing to his three-year-old daughter

24. How old is the speaker in this poem?

    (1) thirty-three
    (2) fifty-three
    (3) sixty-three
    (4) eighty-six
    (5) none of the above

25. What is the best summary of the message the speaker wants to convey?

    (1) Time passes all too quickly.
    (2) Children should love their parents.
    (3) Love endures.
    (4) Children's beliefs change as they grow up.
    (5) The future is unpredictable.

26. What does the speaker expect of Emily's children?

    (1) to look like the speaker
    (2) to know nothing of the speaker
    (3) to know about this poem
    (4) to go into politics
    (5) to feel unloved

WHY IS SHE PAINTING THE GATE?

Painting the Gate

I painted the mailbox. That was fun.
I painted it postal blue.
Then I painted the gate.
I painted a spider that got on the gate.
(5)   I painted his mate.
I painted the ivy around the gate.
Some stones I painted blue,
and part of the cat as he rubbed by.
I painted my hair. I painted my shoe.
(10)   I painted the slats, both front and back,
all their beveled edges, too.
I painted the numbers on the gate—
I shouldn't have, but it was too late.
I painted the posts, each side and top.
(15)   I painted the hinges, the handle, the lock,
several ants and a moth asleep in a crack.
At last I was through.
I'd painted the gate
shut, me out, with both hands dark blue,
(20)   as well as my nose, which,
early on, because of a sudden itch,
got painted. But wait!
I had painted the gate.

May Swenson, "Painting the Gate"

27. To what does the "numbers on the gate" (line 12) refer?

   (1) graffiti
   (2) operating instructions
   (3) a model number
   (4) a street address
   (5) a ZIP code

28. What got painted "because of a sudden itch"?

   (1) her hands
   (2) her nose
   (3) the gate
   (4) the hinges
   (5) a moth

29. Which of the following objects that the speaker painted is least essential to the comic effect of the poem?

   (1) the spider
   (2) her shoe
   (3) the numbers on the gate
   (4) the posts
   (5) the locks

30. What is the speaker's mood in this poem?

   (1) serious
   (2) unhappy
   (3) lighthearted
   (4) ambitious
   (5) worried

31. What can be inferred from lines 1 and 2 about why the speaker painted her mailbox blue?

   (1) That was the only color she had.
   (2) Blue was the color of the gate.
   (3) Blue is associated with the post office.
   (4) Blue is a popular color.
   (5) She was feeling sad.

32. What would the speaker in this poem probably do if she decided to cook for two of her friends?

   (1) serve a gourmet meal
   (2) make enough for ten people
   (3) measure exact portions
   (4) use only blue dishes
   (5) mail invitations to them

Questions 33 through 38 refer to the following poem.

HOW DOES THIS HOUSE GET WARM?

Those Winter Sundays

Sundays too my father got up early
and put his clothes on in the blueblack cold,
then with crackled hands that ached
from labor in the weekday weather made
(5)   banked fires blaze. No one ever thanked him.

I'd wake and hear the cold splintering, breaking.
When the rooms were warm, he'd call,
and slowly I would rise and dress,
fearing the chronic angers of that house.

(10)   Speaking indifferently to him,
who had driven out the cold
and polished my good shoes as well.
What did I know, what did I know
of love's austere and lonely offices?

Robert Hayden, "Those Winter Sundays"

33. Which of the following statements about the father's work can be inferred from the poem?

(1) His job began midmorning.
(2) He worked in an office.
(3) He worked on weekends.
(4) His work required hard labor.
(5) He didn't like his work.

34. Which of the following sets of images is the most important to the main idea of the poem?

(1) night and day
(2) waking and sleeping
(3) warmth and cold
(4) old clothes and good shoes
(5) indifference and anger

35. In the context of this poem, what does the poet mean by "love's austere and lonely offices" (line 14)?

(1) the son's attitude toward the father
(2) the father's dutiful care of the family
(3) the angers that woke the house
(4) the father's attitude toward the weather
(5) rising and dressing alone

36. What is the poet's attitude toward his own past behavior?

(1) He is satisfied with his childhood behavior.
(2) He believes he was right to be angry.
(3) He thinks that teenage indifference is normal.
(4) He regrets his thoughtless lack of understanding.
(5) He thinks he loved his father too much.

37. Which of the following is the best way to describe the meaning of "I'd wake and hear the cold splintering, breaking" (line 6)?

(1) the windows were shattering
(2) the fire was warming the rooms
(3) icicles were forming
(4) glass was breaking
(5) the pipes were freezing and breaking

38. Which of the following can be inferred from the poem?

(1) The boy would go to church.
(2) The boy would go to school.
(3) The father would go to work.
(4) The father would go back to bed.
(5) The boy would go to the office with his father.

WHAT HAPPENED LONG AGO?

Annabel Lee

It was many and many a year ago,
In a kingdom by the sea,
That a maiden there lived whom you may know
By the name of ANNABEL LEE;
(5)   And this maiden she lived with no other thought
Than to love and be loved by me.

I was a child and *she* was a child,
In this kingdom by the sea:
But we loved with a love that was more than love—
(10)   I and my ANNABEL LEE;
With a love that the winged seraphs of heaven
Coveted her and me.

And this was the reason that, long ago,
In this kingdom by the sea,
(15)   A wind blew out of cloud, chilling
My beautiful ANNABEL LEE;
So that her high-born kinsman came
And bore her away from me,
To shut her up in a sepulchre
(20)   In this kingdom by the sea.

The angels, not half so happy in heaven,
Went envying her and me—
Yes!—that was the reason (as all men know,
In this kingdom by the sea)
(25)   That the wind came out of the cloud by night,
Chilling and killing my ANNABEL LEE.

Edgar Allan Poe, "Annabel Lee"

39. How is the special nature of the "love that was more than love" (line 9) emphasized?

    (1) the fact that the lovers were children
    (2) the envy of the angels
    (3) the tragedy of Annabel Lee's death
    (4) the lovers' royalty
    (5) the chilling wind that separated the pair

40. Based on the tone of this poem, what will the speaker most likely do?

    (1) forget about Annabel Lee
    (2) murder Annabel Lee's kinsman
    (3) attend church regularly
    (4) continue to mourn his lost love
    (5) visit Annabel Lee's family

41. If Annabel Lee had survived her chill, what would she most likely have done?

    (1) gone home to her family
    (2) decided to become a nurse
    (3) become the speaker's devoted wife
    (4) become very religious
    (5) decided to be an independent woman

42. What is the poet's primary method for setting the mood in this poem?

    (1) referring to the wind
    (2) capitalizing Annabel Lee's name
    (3) putting the tragedy in the past tense
    (4) repeating "a kingdom by the sea"
    (5) making the cause of death unknown

43. What is suggested about the speaker? He

    (1) never looks back
    (2) has forgotten Annabel Lee's name
    (3) is not affected by life's sorrows
    (4) is ready for another relationship
    (5) still loves Annabel Lee

44. The "sepulchre" (line 19) is <u>most</u> probably what?

    (1) a prison
    (2) a shallow hole
    (3) an elaborate tomb
    (4) a haunted castle
    (5) an open casket

45. In an early letter to a friend, the poet wrote, "I am...a poet—if deep worship of all beauty can make me one." What might this quote help explain about the poem?

    (1) its length
    (2) its sadness
    (3) the narrator's passion
    (4) Annabel Lee's death
    (5) the setting

Questions 46 through 48 refer to the following poem.

WHY IS THIS MAN ALONE?

Bereft

Where had I heard this wind before
Change like this to a deeper roar?
What would it take my standing there for,
Holding open a restive door,
(5)   Looking downhill to a frothy shore?
Summer was past and day was past.
Somber clouds in the west were massed.
Out in the porch's sagging floor
Leaves got up in a coil and hissed,
(10)   Blindly struck at my knee and missed.
Something sinister in the tone
Told me my secret must be known:
Word I was in the house alone
Somehow must have gotten abroad,
(15)   Word I was in my life alone,
Word I had no one left but God.

Robert Frost, "Bereft"

46. Which of the following <u>best</u> describes the time of day and the season of this poem?

    (1) a summer evening
    (2) a fall afternoon
    (3) a fall evening
    (4) a spring afternoon
    (5) a winter evening

47. Which of the following is the <u>best</u> meaning for "sinister" (line 11)?

    (1) threatening
    (2) ugly
    (3) depressing
    (4) frightened
    (5) uneasy

48. Considering the context of the poem, the word "bereft" in the title probably means which of the following?

    (1) deprived of a loved one by death
    (2) failed completely at life
    (3) lost all material possessions
    (4) forgotten everything that matters
    (5) suffered disgrace

Directions: Choose the <u>one best answer</u> to each question.

<u>Questions 1 through 5</u> refer to the following excerpt from a play.

WILL THE GUESTS ENJOY THE PARTY?

(THE COLONEL's valet, BENGTSSON, *wearing livery, enters from the hall, accompanied by* JOHANSSON, *who is dressed very formally as a waiter.*)

(5) BENGTSSON: Now, Johansson, you'll have to wait on the table while I take care of the coats. Have you done this before?

JOHANSSON: During the day I push that war chariot, as you know, but in

(10) the evenings I work as a waiter at receptions. It's always been my dream to get into the house. They're peculiar people, aren't they?

BENGTSSON: Well, yes, I think one might

(15) say that they're a little strange.

JOHANSSON: Are we going to have a musicale this evening? Or what is the occasion?

BENGTSSON: Just the ordinary ghost

(20) supper, as we call it. They drink tea, without saying a word, or else the Colonel talks all by himself. And they champ their biscuits and crackers all at once and all in unison. They sound like

(25) a pack of rats in an attic.

JOHANSSON: Why do you call it the ghost supper?

BENGTSSON: They all look like ghosts. This has been going on for twenty

(30) years—always the same people, always saying the same things. Or else keeping silent to avoid being embarrassed.

August Strindberg, *The Ghost Sonata*

1. Where does this scene <u>most</u> probably take place?

   (1) an attic
   (2) a rich man's house
   (3) a haunted house
   (4) the house of Johansson's regular employer
   (5) a restaurant

2. From this exchange, what might the audience expect later in the play?

   (1) a lively musical event
   (2) a gala dinner party
   (3) the appearance of a ghost
   (4) unusual conversation between people
   (5) a happy ending

3. For what major purpose has the author included Johansson in this scene?

   (1) to be an extra waiter
   (2) as comic relief for Bengtsson
   (3) to introduce him as a primary character
   (4) to make Bengtsson look foolish
   (5) to provide further information about the household

4. Which of the following <u>best</u> explains why Johansson doesn't know about the ghost suppers?

   He has

   (1) worked only on musicale evenings
   (2) never worked in this house before
   (3) been working in this house only during the day
   (4) always thought the people were strange
   (5) only taken care of the coats before

5. Based on the excerpt, which of the following <u>best</u> describes how well Bengtsson knows Johansson?

   He

   (1) doesn't know Johansson at all
   (2) has just met Johansson this evening
   (3) has known Johansson for twenty years
   (4) knows Johansson slightly
   (5) can't remember if he has ever met Johansson

Questions 6 through 9 refer to the following excerpt from a play.

IS BARBARA IN FAVOR OF THIS MARRIAGE?

STEPHEN: I was certainly rather taken aback when I heard they were engaged. Cusins is a very nice fellow, certainly: nobody would ever guess that he
(5)   was born in Australia; but—

LADY BRITOMART: Oh, Adolphus Cusins will make a very good husband. After all, nobody can say a word against Greek: it stamps a man at once as an educated
(10)   gentleman. And my family, thank Heaven, is not a pig-headed Tory one. We are Whigs, and believe in liberty. Let snobbish people say what they please: Barbara shall marry, not the man they
(15)   like, but the man I like.

STEPHEN: Of course I was thinking only of his income. However, he is not likely to be extravagant.

LADY BRITOMART: Don't be too sure of that,
(20)   Stephen. I know your quiet, simple, refined poetic people like Adolphus: quite content with the best of everything! They cost more than your extravagant people, who are always
(25)   as mean as they are second rate. No: Barbara will need at least £2000 a year. You see it means two additional households. Besides, my dear, you must marry soon. I don't approve of
(30)   the present fashion of philandering bachelors and late marriages; and I am trying to arrange something for you.

STEPHEN: It's very good of you, mother; but perhaps I had better arrange that
(35)   for myself.

LADY BRITOMART: Nonsense! You are much too young to begin matchmaking: you would be taken in by some pretty little nobody. Of course I don't mean that you
(40)   are not to be consulted: you know that as well as I do. (Stephen closes his lips and is silent.) Now, don't sulk, Stephen.

George Bernard Shaw, *Major Barbara*

6. What does it mean when Lady Britomart says, "Barbara shall marry, not the man they like, but the man I like" (lines 14–15)?

    It

    (1) shows how unsnobbish she is
    (2) demonstrates her concern for Barbara's welfare
    (3) helps Stephen understand why she approves of Cusins
    (4) implies that she alone knows what is best for Barbara
    (5) takes a positive stand for the liberty of women

7. What is Stephen doing when he replies to his mother's offer to arrange his marriage?

    He is

    (1) being impolite
    (2) making a joke
    (3) encouraging the idea
    (4) showing that he is wary of her interference
    (5) expressing eagerness to find out more

8. According to this passage, which of the following probably makes Adolphus Cusins a good prospect as a husband?

    (1) He is simple, quiet, and refined.
    (2) His parents were Greek.
    (3) He is extravagant.
    (4) He is a Whig.
    (5) He was born in Australia.

9. What response did the author of the play probably intend the audience to have to this scene?

    (1) sadness
    (2) anger
    (3) confusion
    (4) sulkiness
    (5) amusement

WHY IS HELENA'S LIFE DREARY?

HELENA: You hate Alexander without
    reason; he is like every one else, and
    no worse than you are.

VOITSKI: If you could only see your face,
(5)   your gestures. Oh, how tedious your life
    must be.

HELENA: It is tedious, yes and dreary! You
    all abuse my husband and look on me
    with compassion; you think, "Poor
(10)   woman, she is married to an old man."
    How well I understand your compassion!
    As Astroff said just now, see how you
    thoughtlessly destroy the forests, so
    that there will be none left. So you also
(15)   destroy mankind, and soon fidelity and
    purity and self-sacrifice will have
    vanished with the woods. Why cannot
    you look calmly at a woman unless she
    is yours? Because, the doctor was
(20)   right, you are possessed by a devil of
    destruction; you have no mercy on the
    woods or the birds or on women or on
    one another.

VOITSKI: I don't like your philosophy.

(25) HELENA: That doctor has a sensitive,
    weary face—an interesting face. Sonia
    evidently likes him, and she is in love
    with him, and I can understand it. This
    is the third time he has been here since
(30)   I have come, and I have not had a real
    talk with him yet or made much of him.
    He thinks I am disagreeable. Do you
    know Ivan, the reason you and I are
    such friends? I think it is because we
(35)   are both lonely and unfortunate. Don't
    look at me in that way, I don't like it.

VOITSKI: How can I look otherwise when I
    love you? You are my joy, my life, and
    my youth. I know that my chances
(40)   of being loved in return are infinitely
    small, do not exist, but I ask nothing
    of you. Only let me look at you, listen to
    your voice—

HELENA: Hush, someone will overhear you.
(45)   *(They go toward the house.)*

VOITSKI: *(following her)* Let me speak to you
    my love, do not drive me away, and this
    alone will be my greatest happiness!

HELENA: Ah! This is agony!

Anton Chekhov, *Uncle Vanya*

10. What would Helena probably do if she were asked to write an essay?

(1) write clearly and concisely
(2) be too timid to accept the assignment
(3) write about everything except the assigned topic
(4) use a humorous tone
(5) write in a scientific manner

11. Which of the following would be the best title for this passage?

(1) The Doctor's Advice
(2) Man and his Environment
(3) In Defense of Her Husband
(4) The Ignored Suitor
(5) Helena's Hope

12. How does the author intend Voitski to appear in this scene?

(1) as a jolly kidder
(2) as a melodramatic person
(3) as a patient and sincere lover
(4) as rude and insensitive
(5) as a gentle and understanding friend

13. To what is Voitski referring when he says "I don't like your philosophy" (line 24)?

Helena's

(1) reliance on Astroff's opinion
(2) objection to the destruction of forests
(3) belief that the doctor is right
(4) statement that men have no mercy
(5) objection to the compassion of men

14. Which of the following characters are described as friends because they are both unfortunate?

(1) Helena and Voitski
(2) Sonia and Voitski
(3) Helena and Alexander
(4) Sonia and Helena
(5) Voitski and Alexander

WHY DOES THIS PRIEST HAVE TO LEAVE?

O'MALLEY: *(coming forward, sitting down on a sawhorse)* Father, I won't be here at Christmas. *(It takes the old man a moment to grasp the significance of this.)*

(5)

FITZGIBBON: Huh?

O'MALLEY: Well, I was with the Bishop this afternoon and he's transferring me to another parish.

(10) FITZGIBBON: *(coming forward to him, in great alarm)* Oh, you're leaving me? Why, now it never occurred to me that some day you might. But, me boy, what am I going to do without you?

(15) You didn't ask to go?

O'MALLEY: *(smiling)* Oh, no, no, father! As a matter of fact, I asked to stay with you, but *(a little embarrassed)* the Bishop asked me to help him out and I—

(20) FITZGIBBON: *(worried)* But St. Dominic's— what's going to happen?

O'MALLEY: *(calmingly)* Oh, you'll be all right, Father. I wish you could have heard some of the things the Bishop said

(25) about you—it would have done you good. He says you're looking ten years younger. He has all the confidence in the world in you. Now, don't worry, you'll have a new assistant. *(Fitzgibbon*

(30) *comes around the sawhorse and sits down by O'Malley.)*

FITZGIBBON: Well, now, I want to wish you all the success in the world, which I know you'll have. *(Hopefully)* Is it a parish of

(35) your own?

O'MALLEY: Well, no, not—not exactly, Father. You see, this—this church, St. Charles, it's —uh—well, the pastor is getting along in years and things aren't—

(40) FITZGIBBON: *(cocking his head at him)* You mean they're in trouble?

O'MALLEY: Yes. And I'm supposed to go in there and try and help them.

FITZGIBBON: You mean without the old fellow

(45) knowing it?

O'MALLEY: *(smiling)* Uh-huh.

FITZGIBBON: *(innocently, reassuring O'Malley)* Well, now that's a difficult assignment. But it'll work out. You may

(50) have trouble with the old man at first. He may be runnin' off to the Bishop every few minutes, but don't let that bother you. Ah, you'll bring him around to your way of thinkin'.

Frank Butler and Frank Cavett, *Going My Way*

15. The "St. Dominic's" (line 20) Fitzgibbon refers to is probably what?

   (1) small town
   (2) school
   (3) city
   (4) church parish
   (5) priest

16. If O'Malley were a computer scientist, which of the following would he probably be employed as?

   (1) software troubleshooter
   (2) researcher
   (3) hardware developer
   (4) marketing expert
   (5) program designer

17. What are most of the stage directions in this passage intended to do?

   (1) show how well these men know each other
   (2) show how Father Fitzgibbon is getting old
   (3) indicate the tension between the two men
   (4) define O'Malley's personality
   (5) suggest secrecy

18. The final stage direction for Father Fitzgibbon (lines 47–48) is used to suggest which of the following?

   (1) He is simpleminded.
   (2) He is actually describing his own earlier behavior.
   (3) O'Malley is very much in need of assurance.
   (4) He still doesn't understand what is going on.
   (5) He is still a quite competent pastor.

Questions 19 through 22 refer to the following excerpt from a play.

HOW DID THIS MAN DO IT?

BEN: *(as Willy comes toward him through the wall-line of the kitchen)*: So you're William.

(5) WILLY *(shaking Ben's hand)*: Ben! I've been waiting for you so long! What's the answer? How did you do it?

BEN: Oh, there's a story in that.

(Linda enters the forestage, as of old, carrying the wash basket.)

(10) LINDA: Is this Ben?

BEN *(gallantly)*: How do you do, my dear.

LINDA: Where've you been all these years? Willy's always wondered why you—

(15) WILLY *(pulling Ben away from her impatiently)*: Where is Dad? Didn't you follow him? How did you get started?

BEN: Well, I don't know you much you remember.

(20) WILLY: Well, I was just a baby, of course, only three or four years old—

BEN: Three years and eleven months.

WILLY: What a memory, Ben!

BEN: I have many enterprises, William, (25) and I have never kept books.

WILLY: I remember I was sitting under the wagon in—was it Nebraska?

BEN: It was South Dakota, and I gave you a bunch of wild flowers.

(30) WILLY: I remember you walking away down some open road.

BEN *(laughing)*: I was going to find Father in Alaska.

WILLY: Where is he?

(35) BEN: At that age I have a very faulty view of geography, William. I discovered after a few days that I was heading due south, so instead of Alaska, I ended up in Africa.

(40) LINDA: Africa!

WILLY: The Gold Coast!

BEN: Principally diamond mines.

LINDA: Diamond mines!

BEN: Yes, my dear. But I've only a few (45) minutes—

WILLY: No! Boys! Boys! *(Young Biff and Happy appear.)* Listen to this. This is your Uncle Ben, a great man! Tell my boys, Ben!

(50) BEN: Why, boys, when I was seventeen I walked into the jungle, and when I was twenty one I walked out. *(He laughs.)* And by God I was rich.

WILLY *(to the boys)*: You see what I been (55) talking about? The greatest things can happen!

Arthur Miller, *Death of a Salesman*

19. To what is Willy referring when he speaks of the "greatest things" in line 55?

(1) finding his long-lost brother
(2) having two fine sons
(3) remembering his father
(4) hearing about his brother's success
(5) traveling to Alaska

20. Based on the passage, which of the following best describes Willy and Ben's relationship?

(1) They both have sons.
(2) They have different fathers.
(3) They are both single.
(4) Willy is older than Ben.
(5) Ben is older than Willy.

21. In lines 5–6, what does Willy want Ben to explain?

(1) how he succeeded
(2) why he left
(3) where he is going
(4) when he will return
(5) the whereabouts of their father

22. What is the most likely ending for Linda's statement in lines 13–14?

"Willy's always wondered why you—"

(1) never got in touch with him
(2) left him in South Dakota
(3) didn't send him money
(4) went to Africa
(5) never kept books

Questions 23 through 25 refer to the following excerpt from a play.

WHAT IS MR. O'CONNOR LIKE?

AMANDA: That innocent look of your father's had everyone fooled! He smiled — the world was *enchanted!* No girl can do worse than put herself
(5)   at the mercy of a handsome appearance! I hope that Mr. O'Connor is not too good-looking.

TOM: No, he's not too good-looking. He's covered with freckles and hasn't too
(10)   much of a nose.

AMANDA: He's not right-down homely, though?

TOM: Not right-down homely. Just medium homely, I'd say.

(15) AMANDA: Character's what to look for in a man.

TOM: That's what I've always said, Mother.

AMANDA: You've never said anything of
(20)   the kind and I suspect you would never give it a thought.

TOM: Don't be suspicious of me.

AMANDA: At least I hope he's the type that's up and coming.

(25) TOM: I think he really goes in for self-improvement.

AMANDA: What reason have you to think so?

TOM: He goes to night school.

(30) AMANDA *(beaming):* Splendid! What does he do, I mean study?

TOM: Radio engineering and public speaking!

AMANDA: Then he has visions of being
(35)   advanced in the world! Any young man who studies public speaking is aiming to have an executive job some day! And radio engineering? A thing for the future! Both of these facts are
(40)   very illuminating. Those are the sort of things that a mother should know concerning any young man who comes to call on her daughter. Seriously or—not.

(45) TOM: One little warning. He doesn't know about Laura. I didn't let on that we had dark ulterior motives. I just said, why don't you come have dinner with us? He said okay and that was the whole
(50)   conversation.

AMANDA: I bet it was! You're as eloquent as an oyster. However, he'll know about Laura when he gets here. When he sees how lovely and sweet and
(55)   pretty she is, he'll thank his lucky stars he was asked to dinner.

Tennessee Williams, *The Glass Menagerie*

23. Based on her phrase "eloquent as an oyster" (lines 51–52), what word best describes Amanda's attitude toward Tom?

(1) supportive
(2) disapproving
(3) admiring
(4) indulgent
(5) frightened

24. What are the "ulterior motives" (line 47) for the invitation?

(1) to meet Laura
(2) to meet Amanda
(3) to fix the radio
(4) to enjoy Amanda's cooking
(5) to have a good time with Tom

25. What word best describes a man with a "handsome appearance" (lines 5–6), according to Amanda?

(1) loving
(2) ambitious
(3) dangerous
(4) indulgent
(5) envious

HOW DOES IT FEEL TO GROW OLD?

TOM: Oh, Gene, this is damnable. They've lost a suitcase. We had four suitcases.

GENE: Let's see, Dad. There are four there.

(5) TOM: Where?

GENE: Under the others. See?

TOM: That's not ours.

GENE: Yes. Your new one.

TOM: Well, I'm certainly glad you're here.
(10) My mind's like a sieve. *(Low, to Gene)* It's the confusion and worrying about your mother.

GENE: Well, everything's under control now, Dad, so let's go. We'll take a cab
(15) to my apartment, where I've got the car parked, and then I'll drive you out home.

TOM: Your mother can't climb the stairs to your apartment.

(20) GENE: She won't have to. We'll just change from the cab to my car.

TOM: But she might have to use the facilities.

MARGARET: No. No. I'm all right.

(25) TOM *(with a twinkle in his eye…the operator):* You know, if you handle it right, you can get away with parking right out there in front of the station. When I used to come to meet the
(30) Senator…

GENE: I know, but I'd prefer to do it this way. I'm not very good at that sort of thing.

TOM: Well, all right. You're the boss. It's
(35) just that you can get right on the West Side Drive.

GENE: It's easier for me to go up the Major Deegan.

TOM: Rather than the Cross County?

(40) GENE: Yes.

TOM: I don't like to question you, old man, but I'm sure if you clocked it, you'd find it shorter to go up the West Side Drive and—

(45) MARGARET *(annoyed with him):* Father, now, come on. Gene is handling this.

TOM: All right. All right. Just a suggestion.

GENE: Come on, Dad.

TOM: You go along with your mother. I'll
(50) keep an eye on this luggage.

GENE *(trying to be patient):* It will be all right.

TOM *(clenching his teeth and jutting out his jaw, sarcastic):* You don't mind
(55) if I want to keep an eye on my luggage, do you?

Robert Anderson, *I Never Sang for My Father*

26. How does Margaret's attitude toward Gene differ from Tom's?

She is

(1) more supportive
(2) more critical
(3) more aggressive
(4) more interested
(5) more indifferent

27. What does "with a twinkle in his eye…the operator" (lines 25–26) say about Tom?

He

(1) is a thief
(2) is conniving
(3) is easily frightened
(4) worked for the phone company
(5) has tears in his eyes

28. Why is Tom "sarcastic" in line 54?

(1) He feels betrayed by Margaret.
(2) He is anxious about the drive.
(3) He feels defensive about his age.
(4) His mind is like a sieve.
(5) He is trying to get Gene's attention.

29. Why is Margaret "annoyed" (line 45)?

(1) Gene is wrong.
(2) Tom is wrong.
(3) Tom is ignoring her.
(4) Tom is quarreling with Gene.
(5) Gene is being disobedient.

HAS IT BEEN THAT LONG?

MAGGIE: Well, you never know.

MAGGY: No, you never really do. *(Pause.)* You know what? I was a little scared, meeting you again after all these years.

(5) MAGGIE: You were? So was I.

MAGGY: Why were you scared?

MAGGIE: I was afraid it would be awkward and horrible. That our faces would all hurt from fake smiling.

(10) MAGGY: Oh, I hate that.

MAGGIE: Why were you scared?

MAGGY: Because I felt guilty.

MAGGIE: Guilty?

MAGGY: About being the one who got Jim.

(15) Sometimes I worry that I got him under false pretenses.

MAGGIE: What do you mean?

MAGGY: I almost told you about this the other night. Jim and I met at a Fourth

(20) of July parade, did he tell you that?

MAGGIE: Uh-huh.

MAGGY: He was standing there watching the floats, and I kind of sidled over and stood next to him. I remembered him

(25) from school. In fact, I remembered him as your boyfriend. It was surprising to see him standing there by himself all those years later, looking sort of lost and lonely. I just assumed he'd married

(30) you and gone off to become a big shot somewhere—you know, Brown Book Award and all.

MAGGIE: *(Smiling.)* Yeah.

MAGGY: Anyway, there I stood next to Jim

(35) looking at the parade, feeling kind of stupid, and here's what I thought: "If I were Maggie Mulroney right now, what would I say?"

MAGGIE: Uh-oh.

(40) MAGGY: And at that moment a float went by with Gina Lazlo on it. She was looking a little the worse for wear—to tell you the truth she kind of peaked in 12th grade. She was all dolled up as some kind of

(45) overweight sex goddess on a float that said Bigelow Pontiac—she married Robbie Bigelow, did you know that?

MAGGIE: No!

(50) MAGGY: Yes! So here she is on Robbie's float waving a wand, you really had to be there to appreciate the full impact, and I said, "Living proof. You drive 'em off the lot, and they lose their value instantly." *(Maggie laughs.)* Hey, it was

(55) a start.

MAGGIE: I like it.

MAGGY: Yeah, so did he. He looked at me like I'd just arrived on the Planet, one of those "what have we here?" looks,

(60) you know?

MAGGIE: Yeah.

MAGGY: And I felt like a million dollars. Suddenly, with my new personality, I felt so free and liberated. It was great.

(65) But after a while I started to worry. I said to myself, "This isn't really you. Who is it?" Of course I knew the answer right away. It was you.

Catherine Butterfield, *Joined at the Head*

30. Which of these statements about the two women having this conversation can be inferred?

They

(1) know little about one another
(2) have not seen each other in years
(3) have never met before
(4) have recently met
(5) wish they were somewhere else

31. Which of the following best summarizes Maggy's thoughts about Gina Lazlo?

(1) She is envious of Gina's looks.
(2) She is jealous of Gina's marriage to Robbie Bigelow.
(3) She thinks Gina looks foolish.
(4) She thinks Gina's looks have improved since high school.
(5) She likes Gina better than Maggie.

32. Which of the following describes Maggy when she visits with other friends?
She probably

(1) has trouble thinking of something to say
(2) doesn't gossip
(3) listens a lot
(4) talks a lot
(5) prefers to be doing something else

CAN RITA GET A TUTOR?

FRANK: I'll make a bargain with you. Yes? I'll
tell you everything I know—but if
I do that you must promise never to
come back here. You see I never—I
(5)   didn't actually want to take this course
in the first place. I allowed myself to
be talked into it. I knew it was wrong.
Seeing you only confirms my suspicion.
My dear, it's not your fault, just the luck
(10)   of the draw that you got me; but get me
you did. And the thing is, between you,
me and the walls, I'm actually an
appalling teacher. *(After a pause.)*
Most of the time, you see, it doesn't
(15)   actually matter—appalling teaching
is quite in order for most appalling
students. And the others manage to
get by despite me. But you're different.
You want a lot, and I can't give it. *(He*
(20)   *moves towards her.)* Everything I
know—and you must listen to this—is
that I know absolutely nothing. I don't
like the hours, you know. *(He goes to
the swivel chair and sits.)* Strange
(25)   hours for the Open University thing.
They expect us to teach when the pubs
are open. I can be a good teacher
when I'm in the pub, you know. Four
pints of weak Guinness and I can be
(30)   as witty as Wilde. I'm sorry—there
are other tutors—I'll arrange it for
you...post it on...*(He looks at her.)* *(*RITA
*slowly turns and goes out and quietly
closes the door behind her. Suddenly*
(35)   *the door bursts open and* RITA *flies in.)*
RITA *(going up to him)* Wait a minute, listen
to me. Listen: I'm on this course, you
are my teacher—an' you're gonna
bleedin' well teach me.
(40) FRANK: There are other tutors—I've told
    you...
RITA: You're my tutor. I don't want another
    tutor.

Willie Russell, *Educating Rita*

33. Why doesn't Frank want to teach Rita?

   (1) He doesn't want to see her again.
   (2) He doesn't believe he is a very
       good teacher.
   (3) He has too many students already.
   (4) She's too argumentative for him.
   (5) They know each other too well.

34. With which of the following proverbs would
Frank be most likely to agree?

   (1) Don't let the grass grow under your feet.
   (2) Rome was not built in a day.
   (3) Time is money.
   (4) You can't make a silk purse out of a
       sow's ear.
   (5) He who hesitates is lost.

35. What is the effect of Rita's leaving quietly,
then flying back in?

   (1) It makes Frank angry.
   (2) It indicates that Rita has changed
       her mind.
   (3) It shows how important Frank really is.
   (4) It provides a use for the door in the set.
   (5) It shows how confused Rita is.

36. Which of the following attitudes is suggested
by Frank's long, rambling speech?

   (1) uncertainty
   (2) sternness
   (3) affection
   (4) friendliness
   (5) hostility

37. Why does Frank think he is a terrible
teacher?

   (1) He likes the hours.
   (2) He holds classes in the local pub.
   (3) He is very witty.
   (4) He thinks he knows absolutely nothing.
   (5) His students are appalling.

38. Which of the following best summarizes the
reason Rita gives for Frank to be her tutor?

   (1) She enjoys his classes.
   (2) There are no other tutors.
   (3) No one was assigned as her tutor.
   (4) He was assigned as her tutor.
   (5) She has heard how good he is.

IS SILENCE REALLY GOLDEN?

GWENDOLEN: The fact that they did not follow us at once into the house, as any one else would have done, seems to me to show that they have some
(5)   sense of shame left.

CECILY: They have been eating muffins. That looks like repentance.

GWENDOLEN: *(after a pause)* They don't seem to notice us at all. Couldn't
(10)   you cough?

CECILY: But I haven't got a cough.

GWENDOLEN: They're looking at us. What effrontery!

CECILY: They're approaching. That's very
(15)   forward of them.

GWENDOLEN: Let us preserve a dignified silence.

CECILY: Certainly. It's the only thing to do now.

(20)   *(Enter* JACK *followed by* ALGERNON. *They whistle some dreadful popular air from a British opera.)*

GWENDOLEN: This dignified silence seems to produce an unpleasant effect.

(25) CECILY: A most distasteful one.

GWENDOLEN: But we will not be the first to speak.

CECILY: Certainly not.

Oscar Wilde, *The Importance of Being Earnest*

39. Why does Gwendolen want Cecily to cough?

(1) to prepare for being silent
(2) so that Jack will think she is ill
(3) to attract the men's attention
(4) because the men are looking their way
(5) to clear the muffin crumbs from her throat

40. For what purpose does the author have Jack and Algernon whistle?

To

(1) show how musical they are
(2) impress the women
(3) fill some time
(4) demonstrate how casual they are
(5) annoy the audience

41. What does the author probably intend by having Cecily say "They have been eating muffins" (line 6)?

To

(1) have the audience take her seriously
(2) suggest that muffin eating shows repentance
(3) show how insensitive Jack and Algernon are
(4) suggest the time of day
(5) make the audience laugh

42. Given the characters of Gwendolen and Cecily, what will probably happen next in this scene?

(1) The four will sit in silence.
(2) Jack and Algernon will have to beg forgiveness.
(3) Gwendolen will be the first to speak.
(4) The men will ignore the women.
(5) Cecily will burst into tears.

43. Details in this excerpt suggest that all four characters are members of which of the following groups?

The

(1) English upper class
(2) same family
(3) British opera company
(4) same breakfast club
(5) British Parliament

LANGUAGE ARTS, READING

Directions: The Language Arts, Reading Simulated Test consists of excerpts from fiction, nonfiction, poetry, and drama. Each excerpt is followed by multiple-choice questions about the reading material.

Read each excerpt first and then answer the questions that follow. Refer to the reading material as often as necessary in answering the questions.

Each excerpt is preceded by a "purpose question." The purpose question gives a reason for reading the material. Use these purpose questions to help focus your reading. You are not required to answer these purpose questions. They are given only to help you concentrate on the ideas presented in the reading material.

You should spend no more than 65 minutes answering the 40 questions on this test. Work carefully, but do not spend too much time on any one question. Do not skip any items. Make a reasonable guess when you are not sure of an answer. You will not be penalized for incorrect answers.

When time is up, mark the last item you finished. This will tell you whether you can finish the real GED Test in the time allowed. Then complete the test.

Record your answers to the questions on a copy of the answer sheet on page 109. Be sure that all required information is properly recorded on the answer sheet.

To record your answers, mark the numbered space on the answer sheet that corresponds to the answer you choose for each question on the test.

Example:

It was Susan's dream machine. The metallic blue paint gleamed, and the sporty wheels were highly polished. Under the hood, the engine was no less carefully cleaned. Inside, flashy lights illuminated the instruments on the dashboard, and the seats were covered by rich leather upholstery.

What does "It" most likely refer to in this excerpt?

(1) an airplane
(2) a stereo system
(3) an automobile
(4) a boat
(5) a motorcycle

The correct answer is "an automobile"; therefore, answer space 3 would be marked on the answer sheet.

Do not rest the point of your pencil on the answer sheet while you are considering your answer. Make no stray or unnecessary marks. If you change an answer, erase your first mark completely. Mark only one answer space for each question; multiple answers will be scored as incorrect. Do not fold or crease your answer sheet.

When you finish the test, use the Analysis of Performance Chart on page 75 to determine whether you are ready to take the real GED Test, and, if not, which skill areas need additional review.

Questions 1 through 4 refer to the following excerpt from a novel.

WHERE ARE THESE PEOPLE GOING?

Taylor is getting a long, hard look at someone's bald spot. He has reclined his seat to a point where he's closer than a dinner plate, maybe twelve inches from her

(5) face. The top of his head is covered with fine, almost invisible fur that lies flattened in a complicated pattern, like a little prairie swept by a tornado. It reminds Taylor of a theory Jax once told her about, that

(10) humans evolved from some sort of water ape and spent the dawn of civilization in a swamp. Streamlined hair patterns are supposed to be the proof, but Taylor wonders as she stares, Does that mean

(15) we moved through the water headfirst? Could be. Kids move through the world that way, running into things with the tops of their heads. This man has a scar up there, no doubt forgotten through the decades

(20) until now that it's lost its cover.

The pilot comes on the intercom again. He's a chatty one; right after takeoff he introduced himself as "your captain," and Turtle's eyes grew wide. She asked Taylor

(25) if he only had one hand. Now, after mulling it over the whole afternoon, it dawns on Taylor that the only captain Turtle knows about so far is Captain Hook. She may never get on a plane again without

(30) envisioning a pirate at the helm.

Captain Hook now explains they are passing over the Mississippi River, and that if he can do anything to make the passengers more comfortable they should

(35) just let him know. Frankly, although she doubts the captain can help her out here, Taylor doesn't feel comfortable being intimate with a stranger's hair loss. She doesn't even know the top of Jax's head

(40) this well. She's looked at it, but not for three and a half hours.

Turtle is finally sleeping. She seems to be coming down with a cold, and really needed a nap, but was so excited she sat

(45) for hours with her face pressed hard against the window. When the window turned icy cold, even when there was nothing to see but a vast, frosted field of clouds spread over a continent, rutted

(50) evenly as if it had been plowed, Turtle still stared. Everybody else on the plane is behaving as though they are simply sitting in chairs a little too close together, but Turtle is a child in a winged tin box seven

(55) miles above Planet Earth.

Barbara Kingsolver, *Pigs in Heaven*

1. According to the excerpt, for much of the trip Turtle is which of the following?

   (1) scared of flying
   (2) too excited to sleep
   (3) interested in a man's bald spot
   (4) afraid of the captain
   (5) too nervous to talk to her mother

2. Captain Hook is which of the following?

   (1) the pilot's name
   (2) the rest of Jax's name
   (3) the man in the next seat
   (4) Turtle's father
   (5) a character in a pirate story

3. Which of the following best describes the other people on the plane?

   (1) They stare at Turtle.
   (2) They don't understand the captain's announcement.
   (3) They have probably flown before.
   (4) They are all sleeping.
   (5) They seem excited to be flying.

4. What does the narrator mean when she says that "kids move through the world headfirst, running into things with the tops of their heads" (lines 16–18)?

   (1) They often do things without thinking of the consequences.
   (2) They're pretending to swim.
   (3) They look at the ground too much.
   (4) They think too much and become confused.
   (5) They become disoriented when they're tired.

WHY DID JESSIE ORDER A CASE OF SNOWBALLS?

JESSIE: We got any old towels?

MAMA: There you are!

(5) JESSIE: *(holding a towel that was on the stack of newspapers)* Towels you don't want anymore. *(picking up Mama's snowball wrapper)* How about this swimming towel Loretta gave us? Beach towel, that's the name of it. You want it? *(Mama shakes her head no.)*

(10) MAMA: What have you been doing in there?

JESSIE: And a big piece of plastic like a rubber sheet or something. Garbage bags would do if there's enough.

MAMA: Don't go making a big mess, Jessie.

(15) It's eight o'clock already.

JESSIE: Maybe an old blanket or towels we got in a soap box sometime?

MAMA: I said don't make a mess. Your hair is black enough already.

(20) JESSIE: *(continuing to search the kitchen cabinets, finding two or three more towels to add to her stack)* It's not for my hair, Mama. What about some old pillows anywhere, or a foam cushion

(25) out of a yard chair would be real good.

MAMA: You haven't forgot what night it is, have you? *(holding up her fingernails)* They're all chipped, see? I've been waiting all week, Jess. It's Saturday

(30) night, sugar.

JESSIE: I know. I got it on the schedule.

MAMA: *(crossing to the living room)* You want me to wash 'em now or are you making your mess first? *(looking at the*

(35) *snowball)* We're out of these. Did I say that already?

JESSIE: There's more coming tomorrow. I ordered you a whole case.

MAMA: *(checking the TV Guide)* A whole

(40) case will go stale, Jessie.

JESSIE: They can go in the freezer till you're ready for them. Where's Daddy's gun?

MAMA: In the attic.

JESSIE: Where in the attic? I looked your

(45) whole nap and couldn't find it anywhere.

Marsha Norman, *'Night Mother*

5. What do the stage directions suggest about the characters' home?

It is

(1) large
(2) very clean
(3) cluttered
(4) full of beautiful things
(5) old

6. If Jessie were to tell Mama something very unusual, how would Mama probably react?

(1) She would listen carefully.
(2) She would give Jessie only some of her attention.
(3) She would be shocked.
(4) She would go up to the attic and get the gun.
(5) She would get angry.

7. Why does the author have Jessie look for towels, plastic, a pillow, and a gun?

(1) to suggest how untidy Jessie is
(2) as a contrast to Mama eating snowballs
(3) to show how she prepares for Saturday nights
(4) because she is going to dye her hair
(5) to make the audience wonder what Jessie is planning to do

8. In which of the following ways does the author set up the relationship between these two women?

By

(1) a statement in the stage directions
(2) having them argue
(3) having them carry on what are almost two separate conversations
(4) revealing how much Mama is concerned about being out of snowballs
(5) having the two directly say how they feel about each other

9. What does Jessie usually do for Mama on Saturday nights?
   (1) dye her hair
   (2) buy her more desserts
   (3) take her out on the town
   (4) redo her fingernail polish
   (5) get a new *TV Guide*

10. What about Mama can be inferred from this excerpt?

    That she

    (1) is quite attractive
    (2) is fairly lazy
    (3) misses her husband
    (4) wants to go to bed soon
    (5) is a patient person

Questions 11 through 16 refer to the following poem.

WHO IS GOING WHERE?

Even As I Hold You

Even as I hold you
I think of you as someone gone
far, far away. Your eyes the color
of pennies in a bowl of dark honey
(5)   bringing sweet light to someone else
your black hair slipping through my fingers
is the flash of your head going
around a corner
your smile, breaking before me,
(10)   the flippant last turn
of a revolving door,
emptying you out, changed,
away from me.

Even as I hold you
(15)   I am letting you go.

Alice Walker, "Even As I Hold You"

11. When the poet writes "as someone gone far, far away" (lines 2–3), she is preparing the reader for what?
    (1) the image of the bowl of honey
    (2) the idea of a revolving door
    (3) a major tragedy
    (4) a bitter parting
    (5) the last line of the poem

12. Which of the following emotions is the poet probably trying to portray?
    (1) bitter anger
    (2) solemn indifference
    (3) grateful relief
    (4) loving regret
    (5) unequaled joy

13. Which of the following subjects would this poet be most likely to write about in other poems?
    (1) the brutal nature of human beings
    (2) the beauty of a landscape
    (3) understanding in human relationships
    (4) the horrors of war
    (5) the glories of war

14. Why does the speaker describe the other person's hair, eyes, and smile?
    (1) Those are what attracted her to the person in the first place.
    (2) They are what the reader expects to read about.
    (3) They are simple to describe.
    (4) She's thinking about how other lovers will see these things.
    (5) They are all symbols of leaving.

15. Which of the following best describes the eyes referred to in the poem?
    (1) dreamy
    (2) brown
    (3) blue
    (4) shut
    (5) sad

16. Which of the following probably applies to the speaker in the poem?

    She is

    (1) getting ready to leave
    (2) in love with someone else
    (3) totally unselfish
    (4) regretting her decision
    (5) preparing herself to be alone

HOW CAN I REPAY MY LOAN?

Dear Credit Union Member:

We are pleased to inform you that your used car loan request has been approved. We have enclosed an advance of $6347.58. Your first monthly payment, in the amount of $124.93, will be due on the 10th of March, 2001,
(5)   and on the same day of each succeeding month.

No payment coupon book or further notice will be sent to you for this payment. Repayment shall occur through automatic monthly transfer from your Credit Union Share account or deduction from your Credit Union Checking Account or your Super Savers Saving Account.

(10)   YOU MUST SELECT A REPAYMENT METHOD BY FILLING OUT, SIGNING, AND RETURNING THE ENCLOSED REPAYMENT METHOD FORM LETTER.

Whatever repayment method you choose, sufficient funds must be available in your payment account on the day of the loan payment
(15)   transfer. Failure to make funds available will be construed as a loan default and will initiate actions pursuant to the terms set out in the Loan Agreement, including assessment of late fees. After three (3) successive late payments, the vehicle will be repossessed. Twelve monthly payments are required per year.

(20)   Unlike commercial bank plans, your Credit Union allows you to schedule higher monthly payments of any amount over the minimum payment required. You may also make additional payments anytime by mail, in person, on the phone, or through your Internet account by simply transferring monies from your savings or checking account to your
(25)   outstanding loan balance. Each additional payment will be reflected on the loan balance information supplied in your Credit Union Account and Reconciliation monthly statement.

Thank you for allowing us to meet your automotive borrowing needs. Loans to members play an important role in providing the financial benefits you
(30)   enjoy as a Credit Union member.

We appreciate the opportunity to serve you.

Sincerely,

Wilson Markey
Loan Department

(35)   encl: RM form A84A

17. What is the <u>main</u> purpose of this letter?

    (1) to lay out loan repayment options
    (2) to notify the member of loan terms
    (3) to remind the member to make twelve payments per year
    (4) to provide a Repayment Method form letter
    (5) to contrast Credit Union benefits to those of commercial banks

18. If the member fails to keep sufficient funds in the loan payment account for one month, which of the following are probable outcomes?

    (1) repossession of the car
    (2) suspension of Credit Union privileges
    (3) cancellation of the debt
    (4) assessment of a late fee
    (5) reprimand from the Credit Union president

19. Why won't checks be necessary in paying back this loan?

    (1) Payment will be made by credit card.
    (2) Payments will automatically be transferred from the member's Credit Union account.
    (3) The Credit Union will have the payment deducted from the member's paycheck.
    (4) The Credit Union only accepts cash payments.
    (5) Members must pay in person.

20. A brochure for prospective Credit Union members contains the following statements: "The Credit Union is owned and operated by its members. It is a not-for-profit organization exempt from federal taxes. As a consequence, your investments may reap higher yields, and you may enjoy lower interest rates for loans than at commercial banks. You may enjoy advantages unavailable at commercial banks." What aspect of the Loan Letter reflects the advantages claimed by the brochure?

    The

    (1) loan amount
    (2) repayment provisions
    (3) repossession provisions
    (4) approval provision
    (5) monthly payment requirement

21. What document does "encl" refer to in line 35?

    The

    (1) loan agreement
    (2) monthly statement
    (3) coupon book
    (4) default provisions
    (5) Repayment Method form letter

22. What is the "important role" loans play in member services (line 29)?

    (1) They turn credit unions into commercial banks.
    (2) Interest on loans helps pay for member benefits.
    (3) Additional payments may lower total interest accumulation.
    (4) The Repayment Method is inexpensive.
    (5) Loans are not member benefits.

Questions 23 through 27 refer to the following excerpt from a short story.

WHO WAS FRIGHTENED BY A KNOCK AT THE DOOR?

The footsteps came on inexorably, turned out of the road onto the graveled walk, then proceeded quickly and resolutely to the front door. First there was a light, insistent (5) knock, then the latched screen door was heavily shaken.

"He must have a force with him," Minta thought, "he is so bold," and waited for the crash of splintering boards, and braced her (10) body for the thrust of cold steel that would follow. She thought fleetingly of Clenmie, and of her father and mother, and wondered if any sudden coldness about their hearts warned them of her plight.

(15) The screen door shook again, and a woman's voice, old and quiet, called out, "Is there anyone home?" and ceased.

Slowly, cautiously Minta crept to the living room, lifted the side of the green (20) blind. Old Mrs. Beal, her Sunday black billowing in the wind, was homeward bound from dinner with her daughter.

"I saw it was old Mrs. Beal on her way home from her daughter's," she told her (25) father, giving him as much truth as she thought he could handle.

"Minta, you can get to the door fast enough when some of your friends are calling."

(30) "I was busy," replied Minta with dignity. Her father looked at her doubtfully, but he said no more.

Her mother combed out Clenmie's soft, white hair with her rhinestone back (35) comb. "Did you forget to feed Brownie?" she asked.

"Of course I fed Brownie. I'll never forget her. She's my dearest friend."

Against the warm reality of Mrs. Beal's (40) broad, homeward-bound back, the world that had been cold and full of danger dissolved. The dear room; her books, her papers; Clenmie's toys; Mother's tissue cream on top of the piano; (45) the fire sending its lazy red tongue up the chimney's black throat.

She stood warming herself, happy and bemused, like a prisoner unexpectedly pardoned. Then she heard again the click, (50) click she had not recognized. Brownie at the back door!

Jessamyn West, "A Child's Day"

23. What is suggested by the last sentence in this excerpt?

(1) that Minta was hard of hearing
(2) how much Minta loved her pet
(3) that Minta really had forgotten Brownie
(4) that Minta was afraid of Brownie
(5) how much of a liar Minta was

24. What is the effect of putting part of this excerpt in italics (lines 23–38)?

(1) The reader can see into Minta's past.
(2) It shows what Minta's father is thinking.
(3) It shows that Minta is imagining what she will tell her parents.
(4) The reader understands why Minta was so cautious about Mrs. Beal.
(5) It emphasizes how busy Minta was.

25. The "thrust of cold steel" (line 10) that Minta braces herself for refers to what?

    (1) the opening door
    (2) the unlatching of the screen
    (3) a piercing bullet
    (4) a stabbing knife
    (5) the fear in Minta's heart

26. The inexorable footsteps (line 1) really belong to whom?

    (1) a burglar
    (2) a group of forceful men
    (3) Mrs. Beal
    (4) Mrs. Beal's daughter
    (5) a woman in trouble

27. What effect does the sight of Mrs. Beal's back have on Minta?

    (1) She feels lonely.
    (2) She begins to worry about her father and Clenmle.
    (3) She is no longer afraid to be alone in the house.
    (4) She starts to get cold.
    (5) Her world becomes dangerous.

Questions 28 through 32 refer to the following excerpt from an article.

DOES AMERICA STILL EXIST?

For the children of immigrant parents the knowledge comes easier. America exists everywhere in the city—on billboards, frankly in the smell of French (5) fries and popcorn. It exists in the pace: traffic lights, the assertions of neon, the mysterious bong-bong-bong through the atriums of department stores. America exists as the voice of the crowd, a (10) menacing sound—the high nasal accent of American English.

When I was a boy in Sacramento (California, the fifties), people would ask me, "Where you from?" I was born in this (15) country, but I knew the question meant to decipher my darkness, my looks.

My mother once instructed me to say, "I am an American of American descent." By the time I was nine or ten, I wanted to say, (20) but dared not reply, "I am an American."

Immigrants come to America and, against hostility or mere loneliness, they recreate a homeland in the parlor, tacking up postcards or calendars of some (25) impossible blue—lake or sea or sky. Children of immigrant parents are supposed to perch on a hyphen between two countries. Relatives assume the achievement as much as anyone. Relatives (30) are, in any case, surprised when the child begins losing old ways. One day at the family picnic the boy wanders away from their spiced food and faceless stories to watch other boys play baseball in the (35) distance.

There is sorrow in the American memory, guilty sorrow for having left something behind—Portugal, China, Norway. The American story is the story of (40) immigrant children and of their children— children no longer able to speak to grandparents. The memory of exile becomes inarticulate as it passes from generation to generation, along with (45) wedding rings and pocket watches—like some mute stone in a wad of old lace. Europe. Asia. Eden.

Richard Rodriguez, "Does America Still Exist?"

28. If Rodriguez were a teacher, how might he react to his immigrant students?

   (1) hostilely
   (2) sympathetically
   (3) indifferently
   (4) jealously
   (5) admiringly

29. Which word best characterizes the overall tone of this passage?

   (1) amused
   (2) contemptuous
   (3) sad
   (4) exuberant
   (5) passionless

30. What is meant by the reference to "spiced food" in line 33?

   (1) ethnic food
   (2) French fries
   (3) fresh food
   (4) tacos
   (5) hot dogs

31. In lines 42–43, what does the author suggest when he says that children of immigrant children can no longer speak to their grandparents?

   (1) There is a lack of love.
   (2) The grandparents are absent.
   (3) The children don't share their grandparents' language and culture.
   (4) The children are at school.
   (5) The grandparents are too busy learning about their new culture.

32. According to this passage, which of the following is probably true about Richard Rodriguez?
    (1) He is a citizen of a country other than the United States.
    (2) His parents were immigrants.
    (3) His own children will be able to speak the same language as his grandparents.
    (4) His parents wanted to emigrate from the United States.
    (5) He dislikes French fries.

Questions 33 through 40 refer to the following excerpt from a short story.

WHY IS THIS WOMAN UNHAPPY?

I don't like our room a bit. I wanted one downstairs that opened on the piazza and had roses all over the window, and such pretty old-fashioned chintz hangings!
(5) But John would not hear of it.

He said there was only one window and not room for two beds, and no near room for him if he took another.

He is very careful and loving, and
(10) hardly lets me stir without special direction.

I have a schedule prescription for each hour in the day; he takes all care from me, and so I feel basely ungrateful not to value
(15) it more.

He said we came here solely on my account, that I was to have perfect rest and all the air I could get. "Your exercise depends on your strength, my dear," he
(20) said, "and your food somewhat on your appetite; but air you can absorb all the time." So we took the nursery at the top of the house.

It is a big, airy room, the whole floor
(25) nearly, with windows that look all ways, and air and sunshine galore. It was nursery first and then playroom and gymnasium, I should judge; for the windows are barred for little children, and
(30) there are rings and things in the walls.

The paint and paper look as if a boys' school had used it. It is stripped off—the paper—in great patches all around the head of my bed, about as far as I can
(35) reach, and in a great place on the other side of the room low down. I never saw a worse paper in my life. One of those sprawling flamboyant patterns committing every artistic sin…

The color is repellant, almost revolting;
(40) a smouldering unclean yellow, strangely faded by the slow-turning sunlight. It is a dull yet lurid orange in some places, a sickly sulphur tint in others.

No wonder the children hated it! I
(45) should hate it myself if I had to live in this room long.

There comes John, and I must put this away—he hates to have me write a word.

Charlotte Perkins Gilman, "The Yellow Wallpaper"

33. How does the husband's attitude toward the room differ from the narrator's?
    (1) He enjoys the yellow color.
    (2) He enjoys the airiness.
    (3) He prefers to live in a nursery.
    (4) He hates chintz.
    (5) He hopes she can write in the yellow room.

34. What does the narrator's condemnation of the "sprawling flamboyant patterns" suggest about her character?
    (1) She is very particular.
    (2) She has unusual tastes.
    (3) She is artistically inclined.
    (4) She is flamboyant herself.
    (5) She prefers solid colors.

35. What is the consequence to the narrator of John's "prescriptions"?

She

(1) is unhappy
(2) can't think of what to write
(3) doesn't like their room
(4) appreciates everything he is doing for her
(5) is much calmer

36. How does the word "sulfur" in line 43 contribute to the effect of the description?

It

(1) reminds us of the sun
(2) evokes our sense of smell
(3) is slightly metallic
(4) resembles gold
(5) is a confusing image

37. What does the phrase "roses all over the window" suggest about setting?

The

(1) story takes place in the country
(2) story takes place in New York
(3) narrator is living in a hotel
(4) narrator is living in a hospital
(5) story takes place in Italy

38. Earlier in the story, the narrator is forbidden to "work" by those close to her: "So I take phosphates or phosphites—whichever it is, and tonics, and journeys, and air, and exercise, and am absolutely forbidden to 'work' until I am well again." From this passage, why do you think her husband hates for her to write?

(1) He is worried that writing will tax her too much.
(2) He doesn't think women should write.
(3) He is trying to save ink.
(4) He thinks she is writing to companies to get work.
(5) Her sight isn't very good.

39. If the narrator were alive today, what treatment would most likely be recommended for her?

(1) antibiotics
(2) physical therapy
(3) psychotherapy
(4) a strict diet
(5) a heart transplant

40. What is the narrator's attitude toward her husband?

(1) respectful
(2) antipathetic
(3) resentful
(4) sorrowful
(5) passionate

Language Arts, Reading

The chart below will help you determine your strengths and weaknesses on the content and skill areas of the GED Language Arts, Reading Simulated Test. Use the Answers and Explanations starting on page 88 to check your answers to the test.

Directions: Circle the number of each item that you answered correctly on the Simulated GED Test A. Count the number of items you answered correctly in each column and row. Write the amount in the Total Correct space of each column and row. (For example, if you answered 10 nonfiction items correctly, place the number 10 in the blank before out of 11.)

Content \ Cognitive Skill	Compre-hension	Application	Analysis	Synthesis	Total Correct
NONFICTION (Unit 1) General Nonfiction Business Documents	19, 21	28	30, 31 18, 22	29, 32 17, 20	____ out of 11
FICTION (Unit 2) Before 1920 From 1920–1960 From 1960–Present	25, 26 1	39	34, 35, 36, 37 24 3	33, 38, 40 23, 27 2, 4	____ out of 17
POETRY (Unit 3)	15	13	11, 14	12, 16	____ out of 6
DRAMA (Unit 4)	9	6	5, 7, 8	10	____ out of 6
Total Correct	___ out of 7	___ out of 4	___ out of 15	___ out of 14	Total correct: ___ out of 40 1–32 = You need more review. 33–40 = Congratulations! You're ready.

If you answered fewer than 33 questions correctly, determine which areas are hardest for you. Go back to the *Steck-Vaughn GED Language Arts, Reading* book and review the content in those specific areas.

In the parentheses under the heading, the units tell you where you can find specific instruction about that area in the *Steck-Vaughn GED Language Arts, Reading* book. Also refer to the chart on page 3 of this book.

LANGUAGE ARTS, READING

Directions: The Language Arts, Reading Simulated Test consists of excerpts from fiction, nonfiction, poetry, and drama. Each excerpt is followed by multiple-choice questions about the reading material.

Read each excerpt first and then answer the questions that follow. Refer to the reading material as often as necessary in answering the questions.

Each excerpt is preceded by a "purpose question." The purpose question gives a reason for reading the material. Use these purpose questions to help focus your reading. You are not required to answer these purpose questions. They are given only to help you concentrate on the ideas presented in the reading material.

You should spend no more than 65 minutes answering the 40 questions on this test. Work carefully, but do not spend too much time on any one question. Do not skip any items. Make a reasonable guess when you are not sure of an answer. You will not be penalized for incorrect answers.

When time is up, mark the last item you finished. This will tell you whether you can finish the real GED Test in the time allowed. Then complete the test.

Record your answers to the questions on a copy of the answer sheet on page 109. Be sure that all required information is properly recorded on the answer sheet.

To record your answers, mark the numbered space on the answer sheet that corresponds to the answer you choose for each question on the test.

Example:

It was Susan's dream machine. The metallic blue paint gleamed, and the sporty wheels were highly polished. Under the hood, the engine was no less carefully cleaned. Inside, flashy lights illuminated the instruments on the dashboard, and the seats were covered by rich leather upholstery.

What does "It" most likely refer to in this excerpt?

(1) an airplane
(2) a stereo system
(3) an automobile
(4) a boat
(5) a motorcycle

① ② ● ④ ⑤

The correct answer is "an automobile"; therefore, answer space 3 would be marked on the answer sheet.

Do not rest the point of your pencil on the answer sheet while you are considering your answer. Make no stray or unnecessary marks. If you change an answer, erase your first mark completely. Mark only one answer space for each question; multiple answers will be scored as incorrect. Do not fold or crease your answer sheet.

When you finish the test, use the Analysis of Performance Chart on page 87 to determine whether you are ready to take the real GED Test, and, if not, which skill areas need additional review.

Questions 1 through 6 refer to the following poem.

WHAT DOES A POET HEAR IN THE STARS?

When I Heard the Learn'd Astronomer

When I heard the learn'd astronomer
When the proofs, the figures, were ranged
    in columns before me,
When I was shown the charts and
(5) diagrams, to add, divide, and measure
    them,
When I sitting heard the astronomer
    where he lectured with much applause
    in the lecture room,
(10) soon unaccountable I became tired
    and sick,
Till rising and gliding out I wandered off by
    myself,
In the mystical moist night air, and from
(15) time to time,
Looked up in perfect silence at the stars.

Walt Whitman, "When I Heard the Learn'd Astronomer"

1. Why is the astronomer greeted with "much applause" (line 8)?

   (1) He's funny.
   (2) He's respected.
   (3) The show is over.
   (4) The charts are beautiful.
   (5) He's leaving.

2. Based on the poem, which of the following statements is true?

   The speaker in the poem

   (1) understands the stars differently from the astronomer
   (2) is not interested in the stars
   (3) doesn't like the astronomer
   (4) is recovering from an illness
   (5) doesn't understand science and mathematics

3. If the speaker were living today, what hobby might he enjoy?

   (1) computer games
   (2) math puzzles
   (3) basketball
   (4) roller-blading
   (5) bird-watching

4. The "figures" in line 2 might refer to which of the following?

   (1) distances from the sun
   (2) drawings of planets
   (3) characters from books
   (4) astrological signs
   (5) prices of the charts

5. Why does the speaker look at the stars "in perfect silence" (line 16)?

   He

   (1) does not want to wake the others
   (2) is worried that the astronomer will hear him
   (3) does not need to speak
   (4) is afraid that his voice will echo
   (5) is too tired to speak

6. Why does the speaker leave the lecture hall?

   He

   (1) wants to experience nature, not hear about it
   (2) cannot understand the astronomer's lecture
   (3) disagrees with the astronomer's figures
   (4) would like to measure the stars himself
   (5) is not interested in the solar system

Questions 7 through 11 refer to the following benefit document.

WHAT IS AN FSA?
Plan Highlights

Under the Plan, you can establish a Flexible Spending Account (FSA) to help you pay for eligible health care expenses.
(5) Your account is funded through monthly contributions from your salary before taxes are withheld. Contributions are non-refundable and cannot be applied to a subsequent plan year.

(10) A maximum of up to $1,200 and a minimum of $480 can be directed to your FSA for each Plan Year (January 1 through December 31). During the Plan Year, you can receive reimbursement from the
(15) account for your eligible expenses that are not otherwise reimbursed.

Eligibility

You are eligible to participate in the Plan and establish an FSA if you are a full-time
(20) employee.

Eligible Health Care Expenses

To be eligible for reimbursement from your FSA, the health care expenses must be:

(25) • Defined as eligible expenses in Section 213 of the Internal Revenue Code
• Incurred during the Plan Year, and
• Not reimbursed by any employer-sponsored health/dental plan that you
(30) or your spouse are covered by.

Eligible health care expenses include your deductible and co-payment amounts as well as health care expenses not covered under your group medical or
(35) dental plans. These include, but are not limited to, medical expenses (i.e., routine physical exams, rehabilitation); vision expenses (routine eye exams, eye glasses, and contact lenses); hearing

(40) expenses (routine hearing exams, hearing aids, special telephone equipment); dental expenses (dentures and fillings, dental education programs).

Requesting Reimbursement

(45) To be reimbursed from your FSA, simply submit a reimbursement form (Request for Withdrawal) for the expenses you or your dependent incurred. Include proof of the expenses in the form of a bill, invoice, or
(50) Explanation of Benefits form from your group medical/dental plan.

You may submit reimbursement forms as often as you wish. You will be reimbursed for eligible expenses as long as the
(55) requested amount totals $25 or more.

For expenses incurred during the Plan Year, requests for withdrawal will be accepted and processed through March 31 of the following year.

(60) ### When Participation Ends

Generally, your contribution to the FSA ends when your employment terminates. However, you may continue your FSA for the remainder of the Plan Year under
(65) COBRA (Public Law 99-272) by making AFTER-TAX contributions for the remainder of the Plan Year.

For special terms and requirements governing your election to continue
(70) contributions under COBRA, see your Employer.

7. What is the **main** purpose of this document?

   (1) to summarize the plan provisions
   (2) to explain how to submit forms
   (3) to replace the plan document
   (4) to encourage employees to join
   (5) to discourage medical fraud

8. A memorandum to employees summarizing COBRA (Continuation of Benefits) coverage states, "If you are covered by the company's group health plans (medical, dental, and/or flexible spending program), you have the right to retain this coverage if you are terminated (for reasons other than misconduct on your part). Such coverage will continue for 18 months, subject to conditions laid out in the company's plan documents."

   According to the plan document, what is true about the Flexible Spending Account under COBRA?

   (1) It is not affected by termination.
   (2) It continues without change for 18 months.
   (3) COBRA does not cover flexible spending.
   (4) Flexible spending contributions will be after-tax contributions.
   (5) All contributions shall cease upon termination.

9. You submit a bill for over-the-counter remedies that you have taken while ill with the flu. Your request for coverage is denied. Which of the following provides the **most** probable explanation for the denial of coverage?

   (1) Flu is not a routine illness.
   (2) You did not visit your doctor.
   (3) Over-the-counter remedies are not defined as eligible.
   (4) You have submitted bills for less than $25 dollars.
   (5) Over-the-counter remedies are often covered by the regular medical plan.

10. Which of the following is true about contributions to the plan?

    (1) They are not taxed.
    (2) They are limited to $480.
    (3) They can be transferred to another account or saved another year.
    (4) You must pay contributions in a lump sum.
    (5) They can total more than $1,200 if the plan year is extended.

11. For what kind of reader was this document probably written?

    (1) lawyers
    (2) plan administrators
    (3) company board members
    (4) employees
    (5) tax advisors

Questions 12 through 16 refer to the following excerpt from an article.

WHAT DOES THIS ARTIST SEE IN A TREE?

While some artists paint timeless pastoral scenes, Gregory Crane, 37, has invented an ingenuously quirky style of American primitive. His panoramas seethe
(5) with life of the moment—funny little pointy trees, scuttling puffs of clouds, odd tumbledown shacks. "I always responded to landscape," says Crane, who grew up in Washington state and now divides his time
(10) between Brooklyn, N. Y., and southern Vermont. Though his landscapes don't have figures in them, they have a human presence in the objects and small buildings they contain. Recently, says Crane, "I'm
(15) getting into more intimate, closed-in spaces. I've been doing more backyards." Thus, he painted *Mike and Anne's Garden in 1987*. "I like drastic shifts in scale," says Crane, explaining the juxtaposition of the looming
(20) poplar trees and the small blue structure in the background. The painting started with a small oil-and-tempera sketch that he made *en plein air* in his brother-in-law's backyard ("I don't deal with photographs,"
(25) he says). He painted the picture later in his Brooklyn studio. "I like being removed from the scene and figuring it out from my memory and information in the sketch," says Crane. Though the artist sees nature
(30) as animated ("Backyards are like portraits," he says), much of the work's liveliness is due simply to the vigorous, expressive way he paints. The pictures have a strong sense of immediacy. "I allude to the fragility
(35) of nature—a tree bent with age, a structure of this era," he explains. "I deal with the fact that we're in this apocalyptic time."

Cathleen McGuigan, "Transforming the Landscape"

12. What is the meaning of the phrase *en plein air* (line 23)?
    (1) from memory
    (2) with an airbrush
    (3) in his Brooklyn studio
    (4) in an outdoors location
    (5) from a photograph

13. Which of the following quotations from the review best shows how Crane sees a human presence in landscape?
    (1) "I'm getting into more intimate, closed-in spaces."
    (2) "I like drastic shifts in scale."
    (3) "I don't deal with photographs."
    (4) "Backyards are like portraits."
    (5) "I allude to the fragility of nature."

14. How does the reviewer show how Crane "has invented an ingenuously quirky style of American primitive" (lines 3–4)?
    By
    (1) explaining that Crane responds to landscape
    (2) contrasting his work to timeless pastoral scenes
    (3) immediately providing the reader with descriptive images
    (4) referring to the human presence in paintings
    (5) saying that his paintings contain objects and buildings

15. What is the reviewer doing when she refers to the "liveliness" (line 31) and "immediacy" (line 34) of Crane's paintings?
    She is
    (1) linking her conclusion to her introduction
    (2) suggesting that Crane's paintings are too vigorous
    (3) commenting on the fragility of nature
    (4) rephrasing Crane's own remarks
    (5) referring to the shifts in scale

16. What is the meaning of the word "animated" (line 30)?
    (1) cartoonlike
    (2) alive
    (3) factual
    (4) cluttered
    (5) stiff

Questions 17 through 20 refer to the following excerpt from a novel.

WHAT'S ALL THE FUSS ABOUT?

One A.M. Peter and July broke into the captain's cabin. The curtain was pulled across the berth, a heavy blue cambric which also covered the porthole, shutting
(5) out the sun when the captain wanted to sleep. Tentatively Peter pulled back the curtain, possessed by the wild notion that Captain Regan was hiding in his bunk and would leap up and choke him. The berth
(10) was empty, of course. In the hanging locker he found what they were looking for—the wide-brimmed black hat, a pistol and a smooth-bore gun. Peter threw the musket to July and shoved the pistol into
(15) his waistband. Then he picked up the hat, his hands shaking. Suppose it didn't fit? Suppose it was too big and fell down over his eyes blinding him?

"What's so funny?" July asked, a frown
(20) on his handsome face at the absurdity of anything being funny on this menacing day.

"The captain's hat. She's a perfect fit."

"Naturally. You both fatheads."

Peter grinned. "Let's get on back—"
(25) Brother Man interrupted him, sticking his big head through the door. "You better hurry up on deck, Peter. Turno's about to kill Aaron."

With an oath Peter hurried topside. The
(30) burly fireman had cross-eyed Aaron backed up against the rail, choking him. The crew was hollering, "Let him go," but making no move to interfere except for Stretch.

"For God's sake, man," Stretch yelled,
(35) grabbing Turno's arm.

The fireman snatched it free and socked him. The blow dropped Stretch to his knees. Turno lifted Aaron off his feet while squeezing his neck, the deckhand's eyes
(40) rolling around like loose pebbles in his head. "Loose him," Peter yelled running forward. He snatched the pistol from his waistband and reaching the fireman jabbed it into his side. "I ain't fooling,

(45) Turno. Let him go."

Turno released Aaron so suddenly that the man stumbled and fell. Kneeling on the ground and rubbing his neck he blubbered, "He were gon kill me, Peter."

(50) The fireman stared at him with contempt. "You is a lie. I was gonna toss you overboard only half dead and let the sharks finish you off."

Louise Meriwether, *Fragments of the Ark*

17. Which of the following best describes the situation in the excerpt?

It is a

(1) fishing trip
(2) practical joke
(3) shipwreck
(4) trip on a ferry
(5) mutiny

18. When Peter and July broke into the captain's cabin, what did they find?

(1) a blue shirt
(2) two guns
(3) the captain
(4) two hats
(5) a fireman

19. Who is probably the leader of this group?

(1) Peter
(2) July
(3) Aaron
(4) Stretch
(5) Captain Regan

20. Which of the following is suggested by Turno's words and actions?

He is a

(1) weakling
(2) prankster
(3) bully
(4) leader
(5) negotiator

Questions 21 through 26 refer to the following excerpt from a play.

WHAT ARE THESE TWO DOING IN BILOXI?

DAISY: Well, if you could learn to march, you can learn to dance.

EUGENE: Yeah, except if I didn't learn to march, I'd be doing push-ups till I (5) was eighty-three.

DAISY: I'm not that strict. But if it makes you that uncomfortable I won't intrude on your privacy. It was very nice meeting you. Goodbye. *(She starts to walk away.* (10) *She gets a few steps when* EUGENE *calls out.)*

EUGENE: Okay!

DAISY: Okay what?

EUGENE: One two, one two.

(15) DAISY: Are you sure?

EUGENE: Positive.

DAISY: Good. *(She walks over to him, then stands in front of him and raises her left arm up and right arm in position* (20) *to hold his wrist.)*

EUGENE: All I have to do is step into place, right?

DAISY: Right. *(He tucks his cap in his belt and then steps into place, taking her* (25) *hand and her waist and he starts to dance. It's not Fred Astaire but it's not too awkward.)* You're doing fine. Except your lips are moving.

EUGENE: If my lips don't move, my feet (30) don't move.

DAISY: Well, try talking instead of counting.

EUGENE: Okay...Let's see...My name is Gene. *(Softly)* One two, one two...Sorry.

DAISY: It's okay. We're making headway. (35) Just plain Gene?

EUGENE: If you want the long version, it's Eugene Morris Jerome. What's yours?

DAISY Daisy!

EUGENE: Daisy? That's funny because (40) Daisy's my favorite character in literature.

DAISY: Daisy Miller or Daisy Buchanan?

EUGENE: Buchanan. *The Great Gatsby* is one of the all-time great books. Actually, (45) I never read *Daisy Miller*. Is it good?

DAISY: It's wonderful. Although I preferred *The Great Gatsby*. New York must have been thrilling in the twenties.

EUGENE: It was, it was...That's where I'm (50) from...Well, I only saw a little of it from my baby carriage, but it's still a terrific city...What else?

DAISY: What else what?

EUGENE: What other books have you read? (55) I mean, you don't just read books with Daisy in the title do you?

DAISY: No, I like books with Anna in the title too. *Anna Karenina...Anna Christie.* That was a play by O'Neill.

(60) EUGENE: *Eugene* O'Neill. Playwrights named Eugene are usually my favorite...Listen, can we sit down? I've stepped on your toes three times so far and you haven't said a word. You deserve a rest. *(They* (65) *sit)* I can't believe I'm having a conversation like this in Biloxi, Mississippi.

Neil Simon, *Biloxi Blues*

21. When Eugene says "One two, one two" (line 14) as Daisy is walking away, what is he doing?

   (1) counting her steps
   (2) practicing his dancing
   (3) agreeing to dance with her
   (4) making fun of Daisy's dancing
   (5) doing push-ups

22. Which of the following can be inferred from this excerpt?

   Eugene is

   (1) an excellent dancer
   (2) a playwright
   (3) an experienced flirt
   (4) in the army
   (5) very shy

23. Which of the following describes most of the stage directions in this scene?

They are

(1) about what is happening in the background
(2) to show how Daisy and Eugene are supposed to move
(3) to demonstrate why Daisy wanted to dance
(4) too complex to follow
(5) unnecessary

24. Why do the two have a long talk about their names?

Because

(1) they are both named after famous people
(2) they are interested in how people get their names
(3) it is a way to start a conversation
(4) they are seriously interested in literature
(5) all other topics of conversation have been exhausted

25. In this scene, what is the author probably trying to do?

He wants the audience to

(1) feel sorry for Daisy
(2) laugh at the couple
(3) believe in fate
(4) sit on the edge of their seats
(5) want to get up and dance themselves

26. If Daisy and Eugene meet again, which of the following is the most likely?

They probably will

(1) feel very awkward
(2) fall into each other's arms
(3) not speak at all
(4) be cold but polite
(5) be friendly

ARE THESE WOMEN GOOD FRIENDS?

Harriet Smith's intimacy at Hartfield was soon a settled thing. Quick and decided in her ways, Emma lost no time in inviting, encouraging, and telling her to
(5) come very often; and as their acquaintance increased, so did their satisfaction in each other. As a walking companion, Emma had very early foreseen how useful she might find her. In that
(10) respect Mrs. Weston's loss had been important. Her father never went beyond the shrubbery, where two divisions of the grounds sufficed him for his long walk, or his short, as the year varied; and since
(15) Mrs. Weston's marriage her exercise had been too much confined. She had ventured once alone to Randalls, but it was not pleasant; and a Harriet Smith, therefore, one whom she could summon
(20) at any time to a walk, would be a valuable addition to her privileges. But in every respect as she saw more of her, she approved her, and was confirmed in all her kind designs.
(25) Harriet certainly was not clever, but she had a sweet, docile, grateful disposition; was totally free from conceit; and only desiring to be guided by any one she looked up to. Her early attachment to
(30) herself was very amiable; and her inclination for good company, and power of appreciating what was elegant and clever, shewed that there was no want of taste, though strength of understanding
(35) must not be expected. Altogether she was quite convinced of Harriet Smith's being exactly the young friend she wanted —exactly the something which her home required. Such a friend as Mrs. Weston
(40) was out of the question. Two such could never be granted. Two such she did not want. It was quite a different sort of thing — a sentiment distinct and independent. Mrs. Weston was the object of a regard,
(45) which had its basis in gratitude and esteem. Harriet would be loved as one to whom she could be useful. For Mrs. Weston there was nothing to be done; for Harriet every thing.

Jane Austen, *Emma*

27. If Emma were living today, what might her profession be?

(1) teacher
(2) athlete
(3) geographer
(4) writer
(5) photojournalist

28. How did Mrs. Weston's marriage change Harriet's life?

The marriage

(1) forced Harriet into retirement
(2) meant that Harriet left for the city
(3) created a vacuum in Emma's life for Harriet to fill
(4) left Harriet and Emma desolate
(5) taught Harriet to be clever and conceited

29. On what factor does the length of Emma's father's walk probably depend?

(1) his energy
(2) Emma's need
(3) Harriet's availability
(4) the weather
(5) Mrs. Weston's marriage

30. If Harriet were to write about Emma, her words would probably express what feeling?

   (1) guilt
   (2) appreciation
   (3) anger
   (4) jealousy
   (5) pity

31. In line 40, to what does the word "such" in the phrase "two such" refer?

   (1) questions
   (2) homes
   (3) friends
   (4) wishes
   (5) sentiments

32. Which of the following was an effect of Mrs. Weston's marriage on Emma?

   Emma

   (1) felt desolate
   (2) no longer exercised properly
   (3) stopped walking with her father
   (4) became cleverer
   (5) broke off their friendship

33. Which of the following is a reason why, for Emma, her friendship with Harriet cannot replace her friendship with Mrs. Weston?

   Harriet

   (1) is not as clever
   (2) lives farther away
   (3) is less docile
   (4) already has a best friend
   (5) has better taste

34. In line 18, why does an "a" precede the name Harriet Smith?

   To

   (1) show that there is only one
   (2) clarify who Harriet is
   (3) indicate that anyone like Harriet would do
   (4) confuse the reader
   (5) distinguish Harriet from Mrs. Weston

WHAT ARE THE STAKES IN THIS GAME?

"Come on, Paul," said Finnerty, "I've looked Charley over, and he doesn't look so all-fired bright to me. I've got fifty dollars on you with Goldilocks here, and I'll cover

(5) anybody else who thinks Checker Charley's got a chance."

Eagerly, Shepherd slapped down three twenties. Finnerty covered him.

"Bet the sun won't rise tomorrow,"

(10) said Paul.

"Play," said Finnerty.

Paul settled into his chair again. Dispiritedly, he pushed a checkerpiece forward. One of the youngsters closed

(15) a switch, and a light blinked on, indicating Paul's move on the Checker Charley's bosom, and another light went on, indicating the perfect countermove for Berringer.

Berringer smiled and did what the

(20) machine told him to do. He lit a cigarette and patted the pile of currency beside him.

Paul moved again. A switch was closed, and the lights twinkled appropriately. And so it went for several moves.

(25) To Paul's surprise, he took one of Berringer's pieces without, as far as he could see, laying himself open to any sort of disaster. And then he took another piece, and another. He shook his head in

(30) puzzlement and respect. The machine apparently took a long-range view of the game, with a grand strategy not yet evident. Checker Charley, as though confirming his thoughts, made an ominous

(35) hissing noise, which grew in volume as the game progressed.

Kurt Vonnegut, *Player Piano*

35. Which phrase best describes Checker Charley?

   (1) a clever player
   (2) an electronic game machine
   (3) Berringer's perfect partner
   (4) a not very bright checkers player
   (5) Finnerty's gambling pal

36. What does Paul mean when he says, "Bet the sun won't rise tomorrow" (line 9)?
   He
   (1) does not believe the sun will rise
   (2) expects to win the game
   (3) expects to lose the game
   (4) approves of Finnerty's bet
   (5) is eager for the game to begin

37. Why does Berringer pat the pile of money?
   (1) It will make him lucky.
   (2) He believes he will win the money.
   (3) The machine listens to noise at the table.
   (4) The pat closes a switch.
   (5) It acts as a signal to Paul.

38. According to the passage, how is the checkers game turning out?
   (1) Checker Charley is winning.
   (2) Shepherd is losing.
   (3) Berringer is ahead.
   (4) The game is a draw.
   (5) Paul is ahead.

39. Which of the following best describes Finnerty?
   (1) rude
   (2) bored
   (3) confident
   (4) frugal
   (5) cautious

40. Which of the following is the best meaning for "all-fired" (line 3)?
   (1) warmly
   (2) extremely
   (3) flickering
   (4) possibly
   (5) flashy

Language Arts, Reading

The chart below will help you determine your strengths and weaknesses on the content and skill areas of the GED Language Arts, Reading Simulated Test. Use the Answers and Explanations starting on page 88 to check your answers to the test.

Directions: Circle the number of each item that you answered correctly on the Simulated GED Test B. Count the number of items you answered correctly in each column and row. Write the amount in the Total Correct space of each column and row. (For example, if you answered 10 nonfiction items correctly, place the number 10 in the blank before out of 10.)

Cognitive Skill / Content	Compre-hension	Application	Analysis	Synthesis	Total Correct
NONFICTION (Unit 1) General Nonfiction	12, 16		13, 14	15	
Business Documents		9	10	7, 8, 11	_____ out of 10
FICTION (Unit 2) Before 1920		27, 30	28, 29, 31, 32, 34	33	
From 1920–1960	18			17, 19, 20	
From 1960–Present	35, 38			36, 37, 39, 40	_____ out of 18
POETRY (Unit 3)	4	3	1, 2, 5	6	_____ out of 6
DRAMA (Unit 4)	21, 23	26	25	22, 24	_____ out of 6
Total Correct	___ out of 8	___ out of 5	___ out of 12	___ out of 15	Total correct: ___ out of 40 1–32 = You need more review. 33–40 = Congratulations! You're ready.

If you answered fewer than 33 questions correctly, determine which areas are hardest for you. Go back to the *Steck-Vaughn GED Language Arts, Reading* book and review the content in those specific areas.

In the parentheses under the heading, the units tell you where you can find specific instruction about that area in the *Steck-Vaughn GED Language Arts, Reading* book. Also refer to the chart on page 3 of this book.

UNIT 1: Nonfiction

General Nonfiction (pages 4–8)

1. **(2) The odds were against Marshall.** (Analysis) The writer asks what makes Marshall and his lawyers think they could "reverse the tide of segregation" (lines 3–4) and "alter the legal landscape of America" (lines 6–7). Since options (1) and (4) state the opposite, they are incorrect. The writer does not indicate he thinks there is no chance (option 3) or that both sides have an equal chance (option 5).

2. **(4) unequal pay for black teachers** (Comprehension) This information is given in lines 39–40. Option (1) is incorrect because slavery had ended before Marshall's time. Option (2) is incorrect because segregation was the subject of the later case. Option (3) is incorrect because it is not mentioned and is too general. Option (5) is incorrect because states' rights were used to support segregation, the condition Marshall argued against.

3. **(5) great respect** (Analysis) The excerpt says that as a law student Marshall cut classes to hear Davis, something he would do only if he respected Davis. Options (1), (2), and (3) are not supported by the text. Option (4) would not account for Marshall's cutting class to hear Davis.

4. **(3) Marshall's belief in himself and his cause** (Comprehension) This information is stated in line 42. Options (1) and (4) are not true. Option (2) is only referred to rhetorically in the opening question. Option (5) is incorrect because Governor Byrne's actions did not help Marshall's chances.

5. **(1) Horses usually can't do math problems.** (Analysis) Math is usually done only by people, not other animals. There is no support for options (2), (4), and (5); and option (3), though true, is not amazing in itself.

6. **(5) Body language can communicate expectations.** (Analysis) All of the options are true, but only option (5) includes all of the possibilities.

7. **(4) on the radio** (Application) If Hans were performing on the radio, he wouldn't be able to see his audience and get cues from them. All of the other options would allow Hans to see his audience.

8. **(2) to emphasize the scientific validity of the discovery** (Analysis) These words are associated with thinking, especially scientific thinking. There is no evidence for options (1), (3), or (5). No one is absolutely sure what the basis for spoken language is (option 4).

9. **(1) his house** (Comprehension) This is made clear in the text. He takes the figurative phrase literally rather than applying it to actual people as in options (2), (3), (4), or (5).

10. **(3) to defend against** (Comprehension) The idea of protection is repeated here. The other options do not suggest an active protection.

11. **(2) innocent and experienced** (Synthesis) This shows the difference between the child and the adult. One half of each of the pairs in options (1), (3), and (4) is wrong. Option (5) is not a contrast.

12. **(2) A carelessly spoken word can cause harm.** (Synthesis) The whole piece is based on an overheard phrase. Although options (1) and (3) are true, they are not main ideas. Options (4) and (5) are not supported by evidence.

13. **(2) rough** (Comprehension) Living in the open is rough. There is no support for the other options.

14. **(2) fascinated** (Analysis) Although the author is obviously impressed by Snowbird, awed (option 1) is too strong a word. He does not pity the man (option 3), and probably would find nothing to feel confused (option 4) or sad about (option 5).

15. **(3) read the sights and sounds of nature** (Analysis) Although option (1) may be true, it is not suggested here. Option (2) is not true. Options (4) and (5) are not supported by evidence. In option (3), the word read means to interpret.

16. **(4) to sum up Snowbird's worldview** (Synthesis) The quotation does reveal how Snowbird thinks. Option (1) is poor because a quotation doesn't prove that he knew Snowbird. Option (2) is wrong because a quotation isn't needed to state a simple fact. Options (3) and (5) are not relevant to the quotation.

17. **(3) short** (Comprehension) The excerpt says Snowbird was "five feet tall" (line 5). None of the other options are true.

18. **(1) He is eager to continue living and learning.** (Analysis) Snowbird says he is "just beginning to grow" (line 33). This statement makes option (1) the only possible choice. Each of the other options contradicts his words.

19. **(3) Roberto Clemente always played to win.** (Synthesis) Not only does Clemente say he always plays to win (line 47), but the point of the excerpt is to illustrate that fact. None of the other options is the overall idea of the excerpt.

20. **(2) He was a close friend of Clemente.** (Comprehension) This information is stated in lines 6–7. Therefore, all the other options are incorrect.

21. **(4) He took the game seriously.** (Synthesis) Wearing his uniform meant the softball game was just as important as a big league game. Options (1) and (5) are incorrect because they imply attitudes that are not supported by the excerpt. Option (2) is not true. Option (3) is not mentioned in the excerpt.

22. **(1) intense** (Analysis) Everything in the excerpt shows that Clemente took all games seriously and always played to win. Options (2), (3), and (4) are not supported by the excerpt. Option (5) is true but not the best description.

Reviews of Visual Arts (pages 9–13)

1. **(2) Topics** (Analysis) In lines 27–32, Topics is alluded to as an information source, specifically for house training. Options (1), (3), and (4) are features of the program but are not ways of finding information. Option (5) would not lead to the necessary information.

2. **(2) The shape suggests the subject.** (Analysis) The answer relates graphical interface to the purpose of the software. The remaining options are either untrue or unsupported by the text.

3. **(2) You can't find out if a dog is good-natured.** (Analysis) The reviewer specifically complains about lack of information about dog personality. Option (1) has no support in the review. Option (3) can be answered by looking at the dog's picture. Options (4) and (5) allude to information that is present in the entries.

4. **(3) search tool** (Analysis) Lines 23–26 indicate that a search for suitable dogs will take place. Options (1), (2), and (5) refer to other aspects of the CD-ROM. Option (4) is untrue.

5. **(2) a toolbar** (Comprehension) This information is provided in lines 15–16. The other choices are all features of the software but not the means of navigation.

6. **(5) an authority on Rubens** (Comprehension) The lecturer has written books on Rubens. He is from Oxford University (option 2). Option (3) is the occasion for the talk. Rubens, sometimes a biblical illustrator (option 4), was the subject of the talk.

7. **(2) as an example of how Rubens included contemporary portraits in his paintings** (Analysis) The archduchess, a contemporary of Rubens, is found in an altarpiece. Option (1) refers to how Rubens humanized his subjects. Options (3) and (4) are too general. Option (5) may be true, but the reviewer is not the lecturer.

8. **(2) a food vendor and a senator** (Application) Rubens used both important people and ordinary people in his paintings. Options (1), (3), and (4) would be more likely in the 17th century. There is no support for option (5).

9. **(2) Rubens conveyed people's humanity** (Synthesis) Rubens didn't stylize his portraits but painted people realistically, apparently an unusual practice. None of the other options are supported by information in the text.

10. **(3) symbol** (Analysis) The parenthetical comment refers to a scientific symbol that the reviewer isn't familiar with. The other options cannot be inferred from the context.

11. **(1) casual** (Synthesis) The ironic reference to the meaning of the term RedShift in the first paragraph, the language of the parenthetical comments in the second paragraph, and the use of the word stuff in lines 24 and 33 are all examples of a casual style. There is no evidence to support any of the other options.

12. **(3) likes the software** (Synthesis) The reviewer uses words like "wonderful" and "interesting" to describe some of the features. He points out some of the drawbacks of the software, but his overall opinion of it is positive, so Option (1) is incorrect. All of the other options are contradicted by information in the review.

13. **(1) bright teenagers** (Analysis) The reviewer associates "Star Wars" with the "intellectual and emotional level of a bright teenager." (lines 33–34) All other options are discounted or irrelevant.

14. **(3) They are amused at themselves for taking the film seriously.** (Analysis) The smile suggests ironic self-awareness on the part of the analyzers. Options (1) and (2) are unlikely; options (4) and (5) are either irrelevant or not suggested by the evidence.

15. **(2) a successful formula** (Expanded Synthesis) Ebert describes the formula and attributes the success of other similar films to it. Options (1) and (3) are not addressed in the passage. Options (4) and (5) result from faulty inference.

16. **(3) It is a brilliant special-effects movie with a powerful story.** (Synthesis) The reviewer praises both the special effects and the story line, discounting option (2). The other options are negative and cannot represent a positive review.

17. **(5) cannot be determined** (Analysis) All references are to Dern's role as written in the movie, not to his performance. Consequently, all other options cannot be inferred.

18. **(2) a bit too fast** (Analysis) The reviewer notes the movie's uncomfortably fast pace, but his reaction is both critical and admiring (the "gait carries us with it"). Option (1) does not account for the criticism of Thornton's eagerness "to move things along." The remaining options are incorrect.

19. **(1) the last scene** (Comprehension) The only element to receive criticism is the "coda" or ending. All other options are either incorrect or cannot be inferred.

Business Documents (pages 14–18)

1. **(2) to summarize the policy coverages** (Synthesis) The first paragraph refers to a "quick reference." There is no evidence for options (1), (4), and (5), and option (3) is specifically discounted.

2. **(4) no reimbursement** (Comprehension) Lines 35–40 provide this information. All other options are incorrect.

3. **(4) to start setting up teams and scheduling** (Synthesis) This option is the only possibility after all other options are eliminated. Options (1) and (5) are too specific. Option (3) is irrelevant. Option (2) cannot be inferred.

4. **(2) straightforward and matter-of-fact** (Synthesis) This option is the only possibility after all other options are eliminated. Options (1) and (5) are eliminated because of the memorandum's diction and relative brevity. Options (3) and (4) are eliminated because of word choice.

5. **(5) Dan will consider hiring consultants a necessary expense in this case.** (Expanded Synthesis) This option can be inferred from the section on Staffing. Option (1) is unlikely, since Ralph has been told to hire consultants. Options (2) and (3) cannot be inferred. Option (4) is contradicted by Ralph's statements.

6. **(4) return the title to the Title Office** (Comprehension) This option is explicitly stated in lines 21–25. All other options are incorrect or irrelevant.

7. **(1) to help title owners care for their title** (Synthesis) This option can be inferred from the entire insert. Options (2), (3), and (5) are too specific. Option (4) is irrelevant.

8. **(4) Your title proves that you own the vehicle.** (Analysis) This option is stated in line 2. Options (1), (2), and (5) are either incorrect or cannot be inferred. Option (3) may be true, but not sufficiently relevant.

9. **(2) concise** (Synthesis) This option can be inferred from the entire document. Options (1) and (3) can be eliminated on the basis of word choice. Options (4) and (5) can be eliminated on the basis of length.

10. **(3) amateur home repairers** (Analysis) This option must be inferred from the word choice and level of detail. Options (1) and (4) cannot be inferred. Options (2) and (5) are both irrelevant and too limited.

11. **(4) giving a sequence of steps** (Synthesis) This option is correct for any set of instructions. All other options are either inadequately descriptive or incorrect.

12. **(3) Extenders can be placed on either side in a sash window.** (Comprehension) This option is the only correct response. All other options either cannot be inferred or are incorrect.

13. **(2) They help readability.** (Analysis) This option is the only correct response. All other options either cannot be inferred or are incorrect.

14. **(3) a faulty TV speaker** (Application) Only Option (3) is covered, implicit by coverage of televisions. All other options are either explicitly excluded or irrelevant.

15. **(2) to provide legal guidelines for claims** (Synthesis) This option can be inferred from the entire document. Options (1) and (3) cannot be inferred. Options (4) and (5) are either too limited or irrelevant to the warranty.

UNIT 2: Fiction

Before 1920 (pages 19–26)

1. **(3) marriage** (Analysis) The following sentence makes it clear that the words refer to Aylmer's marriage. All other options are not supported by information in the passage.

2. **(2) He would never leave science completely.** (Analysis) The word "weaned" implies a complete break. Options (1), (4), and (5) cannot be inferred. Option (3) is incorrect.

3. **(3) to be god-like** (Application) This answer can be inferred from Aylmer's passion for science and the allusion to making new worlds. Options (1) and (5) are too narrow. Options (2) and (4) are not supported by the passage.

4. **(3) a scientific treatise** (Application) This option fits with Aylmer's character. None of the other options can be inferred from the excerpt.

5. **(3) He is impenetrable.** (Analysis) The image suggests a wall. All other options are either incorrect or cannot be inferred from the excerpt.

6. **(2) The speaker emphasizes facts over any emotion.** (Expanded Synthesis) The narrator's devaluing of emotion foreshadows his daughter's loveless marriage. Options (1), (3), and (4) cannot be inferred. Option (5) is irrelevant.

7. **(1) The neckcloth is tight.** (Analysis) The allusion is to strangling. All other options are either irrelevant or incorrect.

8. **(2) mathematics** (Application) Only this option reflects the speaker's admiration of facts over feeling.

9. **(1) Don Quixote has a vivid imagination.** (Analysis) Don Quixote imagines that the windmills are giants he must slay. Options (2) and (4) are incorrect because, while they both are looking at the windmills, Sancho Panza sees them literally, and Don Quixote sees them as adversaries in an imaginative adventure. Even though Don Quixote says to Sancho Panza "if you are afraid," there is no evidence that Sancho is afraid (option 3). Option (5) is incorrect because Don Quixote says he will fight the giants even though they are numerous and huge.

10. **(3) He would be unconcerned.** (Application) In this excerpt, Don Quixote is ready to go against "thirty or more monstrous giants." Options (1) and (4) are incorrect because they are the opposite of what the excerpt shows about Don Quixote. Options (2) and (5) are incorrect because in this excerpt Don Quixote ignores Sancho Panza's explanation and is determined to proceed without him.

11. **(1) worried about finding an intruder in his home** (Analysis) Scrooge is checking to be sure no one is hiding and to see that nothing has been moved. Options (2) and (5) are wrong because there is no evidence for either of these. He is clearly familiar with how and where everything should be, so options (3) and (4) are wrong.

12. **(4) Double-Checking** (Application) The passage suggests that Scrooge is nervously making sure all is in order, therefore eliminating option (5). Option (1) has no support, and there is no evidence of a city (option 2). Nothing has happened yet, so option (3) is wrong.

13. **(3) She is on the verge of adulthood.** (Analysis) The words suggest an adolescent awakening. Options (1), (4) and (5) are true about Sylvia, but do not explain the quote. Option (2) is incorrect.

14. **(1) They both like birds.** (Analysis) This answer can be inferred from Sylvia's empathy with the birds and her own assertion that the woodsman likes birds. Options (2) and (3) are wrong about one character or the other. Option (4) is disproved by the information in the passage. Option (5) cannot be inferred.

15. **(2) They are searching for a white heron and don't want to startle it.** (Analysis) If the heron has eluded them (lines 34–35), they must have been searching for it. Option (1) sounds likely but is contradicted by lines 6–8. Options (3), (4), and (5) cannot be inferred from the passage.

16. **(5) reciting the multiplication tables** (Comprehension) "7 times 9" is part of the multiplication tables. The class is obviously reciting, so options (1) and (2) are wrong. Options (3) and (4) take place after Demi overhears Nat.

17. (1) what the boys have learned in school (Comprehension) There is no evidence that the boys have ever heard about option (2). Option (3) reflects a confusion about the word *stores*. The lesson in learning was from Mr. Bhaer (option 4). There is no support for option (5).

18. (3) because he realizes he already has been able to learn something (Analysis) Options (1) and (2) are wrong because they don't occur until after Nat decides. Options (4) and (5) are wrong because Nat doesn't believe them either, but he has learned how to be patient and how to fiddle.

19. (5) sympathetic (Analysis) There is no support for options (1), (2), and (4). Although option (3) could be true, it is not the main quality that is demonstrated.

20. (2) how well Nat played the fiddle (Analysis) The reader has no way of knowing everything that Mr. Bhaer included in his "lesson in learning." However, when Mr. Bhaer had finished, we are told that the other boys warmly received Nat, "the chap who fiddled so capitally."

21. (2) show that Demi was carried away (Analysis) Demi is so enthusiastic about helping Nat that he stumbles over his words. The other options cannot be inferred from the passage.

22. (4) confident (Analysis) The young woman's behavior and words exude confidence. Options (1) and (5) are incorrect. Options (2) and (3) cannot be inferred from the excerpt.

23. (2) to help us judge their characters (Comparison/Contrast—Analysis) The description encourages us to make evaluations based on common traits. Options (1) and (3) cannot be inferred. Option (4) is attractive, but too general a statement. Option (5) is not relevant to the comparison.

24. (4) embarrassed by the handcuffs (Comprehension) The option remains after all others are eliminated. Options (1) and (3) are possible, but difficult to infer. Options (2) and (5) cannot be inferred.

25. (5) Miss Fairchild likes Mr. Eaton. (Analysis) This option is suggested not only by the smile, but also by Miss Fairchild's character. She is unlikely to smile at someone she does not like. The remaining options are either impossible to infer or contradicted by the text.

26. (4) stubborn (Analysis) Bartleby's continual refusal to switch tasks indicates inflexibility. The other options cannot be inferred from the excerpt.

27. (5) word processor (Application) Bartleby's job entails transcribing, as described in the first paragraph. The other options do not fit the evidence.

28. (3) Bartleby's refusal to help is completely mystifying. (Expanded Synthesis) The quote helps explain the narrator's attitude toward Bartleby's behavior. The other options do not explain the earlier assertion or cannot be inferred.

29. (3) north, toward the North Pole (Analysis) The allusion to higher latitudes and ice make this answer clear. In addition, we must presume that the letter writer begins from England. The other options are incorrect on the evidence.

30. (1) would be important (Analysis) This answer can be inferred from the paragraph. Options (2) and (3) do not make sense in the context of the letter. Options (4) and (5) are eliminated by the writer's intent.

31. (2) captain (Comprehension) The letter-writer refers to "my men," and his position can be inferred from those words. The other options are eliminated by the evidence in the letter.

32. (2) bold (Analysis) This answer can be inferred by the tone and language of the letter, as well as the writer's intent to make a dangerous journey. Options (1) and (5) might be true, but they cannot be inferred from the excerpt.

33. (5) reassure her (Synthesis) This answer can be inferred by the tone and statements in the letter. Options (1) and (4) cannot be inferred. Options (2) and (3) are contradicted by the content of the letter.

Fiction

From 1920–1960 (pages 27–34)

1. (2) We feel that the doctor is deceiving himself and the patient. (Analysis) The doctor's statement is juxtaposed with a clear indication that the machine is not working. The other options are either incorrect or irrelevant.

2. (3) The new pavilions might have been added since the war. (Analysis) All the patients in the new pavilion seem to be war veterans. Options (2), (4), and (5) cannot be inferred. Option (1) is not supported by the evidence.

3. (5) The machine and a tricycle move in the same way. (Analysis) This option is suggested in the passage. Options (1) and (3) are irrelevant. Options (2) and (4) seem unlikely.

4. **(1) He wrote from experience.** (Expanded Synthesis) This option remains as all others are eliminated. Options (2), (3), and (5) are unsupported by the evidence. Option (4) is true, but not relevant.

5. **(3) storm out of the room** (Application) Braggioni is passionate and conceited, so this behavior is consistent with his character. Options (1) and (5) are completely out of character. Options (2) and (4) are mild reactions and unlikely, given his temper.

6. **(1) He prefers to sing.** (Comprehension) Braggioni is undeterred from his singing. The other options are either irrelevant or cannot be inferred.

7. **(2) We learn that Laura really appreciates beautiful music.** (Comparison/Contrast—Analysis) Laura's very different reaction to the two singers tells us much about her. Options (1) and (4) are untrue. Options (3) and (5) cannot be inferred from the excerpt.

8. **(3) an algebra teacher** (Comprehension) This is stated in the text. Option (1) is not the best description even though it is clear that the narrator once knew Sonny and still cares about him. There is not sufficient support for options (2), (4), or (5).

9. **(1) The narrator is extremely worried about a person he had once known well.** (Synthesis) The narrator's agitation and the sense of sorrow and dread is clear throughout the excerpt. Options (4) and (5) are not suggested by this passage. Option (2) is wrong as the ice is not real. Option (3) is the opposite of what is stated.

10. **(3) to have changed physically because of drug use** (Analysis) This is suggested in the last few lines. Options (1), (2), and (5) have no support in the excerpt. Option (4) is probably the opposite of reality.

11. **(2) as a vivid example of how distressed the narrator is** (Analysis) The ice is a metaphor, a comparison that helps the reader understand how the teacher is feeling. Option (1) is not true. Options (3) and (4) are irrelevant. Option (5) is unlikely.

12. **(4) regret for what Sonny once was like** (Analysis) The narrator remembers Sonny's gentleness and the bright look on his face and is saddened at what he has become. However, he is not disgusted (option 1) or afraid (option 2). He certainly is not relieved (option 3) or happy (option 5) that Sonny has been caught.

13. **(5) before he got to school** (Comprehension) This information is given in lines 1–3. Therefore, all the other options are incorrect.

14. **(2) She is unstoppable.** (Comprehension) The allusion to the truck reveals her stubborn character. The other options either cannot be inferred or are irrelevant.

15. **(4) She is changing the subject.** (Analysis) Mrs. Freeman's irrelevant question is an attempt to deflect the accusation that she is wrong. All other options cannot be inferred from the excerpt.

16. **(2) stick to her position** (Application) She is difficult to deter or deflect. The other options are unlikely, given the evidence.

17. **(4) stubborn** (Analysis) She is clearly inflexible. The other options cannot be inferred from the excerpt.

18. **(4) He came to see George's mother.** (Comprehension) Eugene states this information in lines 25–26. Therefore, all the other options are incorrect.

19. **(3) He didn't want his mother to know Eugene had come.** (Analysis) Based on George's message to Eugene, it can be assumed that George knows that Eugene is at the door and wants to send him away before his mother knows Eugene has arrived. For this same reason, option (1) is incorrect. Options (2), (4), and (5) all deal with the housemaid, and there is no evidence that George's motivation for answering the door had anything to do with her.

20. **(5) He didn't expect any fuss.** (Analysis) Although Eugene seems surprised that George answers the door, he nevertheless says why he has come and clearly doesn't expect George to reply as he does. Therefore, options (1) and (3) are incorrect. Option (2) is not indicated by anything in the text and contrary to the usual procedure of Mary answering the door. Option (4) is incorrect for two reasons: He clearly didn't expect George to answer since Mary usually did so; based on the subsequent conversation it is logical to assume that Eugene and George were not on good terms and George would not have invited Eugene in.

21. **(1) refined** (Analysis) George and Eugene speak formally and remain conventionally polite even when they get angry. Therefore, options (2), (3), and (5) are incorrect. Even though Eugene begins the encounter in a friendly manner (option 4), he soon changes in response to George, who is unfriendly from the beginning.

22. **(3) Uncle Buddy is after the dogs that are chasing a fox around the house.** (Comprehension) Option (1) implies that Uncle Buddy is in control of what is happening. Options (2) and (5) limit the chase to the kitchen and, along with option (4), confuse the actual order of who is chasing whom.

23. **(4) The chase had led through the woodpile by the chimney.** (Analysis) Option (4) is supported by the sticks of firewood that get involved in the chase. There is no evidence for option (1). The noises in options (2) and (3) would not create the sound described. Option (5) suggests that Uncle Buddy would be hurt, but he isn't. Also note the word like meaning as if; nothing actually happened to the chimney.

24. **(5) part of the family** (Analysis) Although options (1) and (4) may be true, there is no support for these two opinions. There is no evidence for option (3). The fact that there is a dog's room makes option (2) wrong and suggests that option (5) is correct.

25. **(2) putting all the action in one long sentence** (Analysis) The one long sentence builds clause on top of clause to create an impression of breathlessness. Option (1) comments on the chase, but doesn't contribute to it. No one's reactions, as suggested by option (3), are described. Options (4) and (5) are merely part of the chase.

26. **(2) a ship's horn** (Comprehension) This information is stated in lines 15–16. Option (1) is incorrect because no fire is mentioned. Although a dog (option 3), a fox (option 4), and a chimney (option 5) are mentioned, they are not compared to Uncle Buddy's bellowing.

27. **(2) It explains the slapstick nature of the chase.** (Expanded Synthesis) The quote is relevant to the comic element of the excerpt. Option (1) is inconsistent with the quote. Options (3), (4), and (5) are either irrelevant or cannot be inferred.

28. **(2) He does not have formal education.** (Analysis) The mistake in usage ("a" for "an") and other missteps suggest a man with little schooling. Options (1), (4), and (5) may be true, but are irrelevant to the quote. Option (3) seems unlikely and is not supported by the evidence.

29. **(4) It is ten o'clock at night.** (Analysis) The lateness of the hour is evidenced in the excerpt only by this detail about darkness. Options (1) and (3) may be true, but cannot be inferred. Options (2) and (5) are contradicted by the evidence in the excerpt.

30. **(3) too frightened** (Analysis) This option can be inferred through the details of "caved-in voice" and the evidence of fear as she calls her brother. Options (1) and (4) are not supported by the evidence. Options (2) and (5) are untrue.

31. **(1) It happened fifteen years ago.** (Comprehension). The words "fifteen years" (lines 58–59) answer the question posed at the beginning of the paragraph, "How long ago?" The remaining options are thus all incorrect.

32. **(2) detailed** (Synthesis) The extremely detailed description of the pass-play predominates in the excerpt. The other options are incorrect.

Fiction

From 1960–Present (pages 35–43)

1. **(2) hard** (Analysis) Miss Dulcie treats the narrator harshly. Options (1), (3), and (5) are incorrect, and option (4) cannot be inferred.

2. **(3) Her trip is an important event.** (Analysis) No evidence exists to suggest that the narrator is rich (option 1). The trip is clearly central to her future life. Options (2) and (4) cannot be inferred. Option (5) is unlikely, given Miss Dulcie's treatment of the narrator.

3. **(4) She accepted it.** (Comprehension) The narrator explains that such treatment was customary, and, in lines 38–41, makes clear her acceptance at the time. Only later did she feel angry. Options (1), (2), and (3) are incorrect. Option (5) cannot be inferred.

4. **(2) walk on by** (Application) The narrator has already turned her back on Miss Dulcie. All options except (4) are implausible. Option (4) is unlikely, given the last sentence.

5. **(4) Bert and Manny are longtime friends.** (Comprehension) The text says Bert and Manny had been "friends for twenty years" (lines 4–5). Therefore, all the other options are incorrect.

6. **(3) funeral** (Comprehension) This information is given in lines 14–22. Option (2) is incorrect because Manny didn't feel any grief, although he knew he should. The other options are not supported by the text.

7. **(4) special events director** (Application) Manny is very interested in planning Bert's funeral and making it memorable. Options (1) and (3) are not likely since he displays little sympathy. Option (2) is incorrect because he doesn't indicate any interest in medicine. Option (5) is incorrect because there is no information to support his possible writing skills.

8. **(1) She uses her ability to protect herself.** (Expanded Synthesis) This option includes information supplied by the supplemental passage. Sometimes, the narrator runs from trouble. Options (2), (3), (4), and (5) cannot be inferred.

9. **(4) weightless** (Comprehension) The narrator switches back to feeling weightless at the exact point of the pistol shot. The remaining options are either wrong or cannot be inferred.

10. **(3) She feels as if she can beat anyone.** (Analysis) The phrase "even her father" suggests that her father is her strongest competitor. If she can beat him, she can beat anyone. The remaining options are either wrong or cannot be inferred.

11. **(5) old Luze** (Comprehension) "He" also refers to himself as "old Luze." There is no basis for options (2) and (4). Option (1) is grammatically impossible. That "we" watched him wave goodbye eliminates option (3).

12. **(4) schoolchildren** (Analysis) Old Luze has made them both promise to go back to school. There is no evidence for the other options.

13. **(1) to emphasize the suspense of waiting** (Analysis) Option (1) refers to the tension of waiting for the train. The ideas are not complex (option 5), nor is there a reason for contrast with the dialogue (option 4) or the first sentence (option 3). Option (2) is wrong because dialogue has nothing to do with length.

14. **(2) getting on the train** (Comprehension) It refers to the train and snag means catch, or get on, which Luze does before he waves (option 1). There is no support for options (3), (4), or (5).

15. **(3) concern** (Analysis) The words suggest parental concern. Options (1), (4), and (5) have no support in the excerpt. Option (2) is too strong and not the best choice.

16. **(2) because Lee wasn't interested in football** (Comprehension) Options (1) and (4) are contradicted in the text. Option (3) has no support. Option (5) is wrong because the narrator contrasts savvy with sense. Option (2) is part of the example for this contrast.

17. **(2) Lee was smart, but baffled by football scoring.** (Comprehension) This is the only option supported by direct evidence. The narrator thinks option (3) may be possible someday, but only with practice.

18. **(3) an intellectual talking bird** (Comprehension) Schwartz, clearly a bird, reads to the boy and appears to have fairly refined taste. He is not a pet (option 1), is unwelcome only to the father (option 2), and is a firm tutor (option 4). He may like chess (option 5), but we don't know how much.

19. **(3) slightly fanciful** (Synthesis) Options (1) and (5) are both too extreme. There is no evidence for either option (2) or option (4). The scene is almost believable.

20. **(3) He wants to end the interrogation.** (Comprehension) The narrator's motivation is explained in lines 27–29. The other options are not supported by the text.

21. **(1) polite** (Analysis) Throughout the passage, the narrator behaves politely. The remaining options have no support in the excerpt.

22. **(2) at school** (Application) Logically, he will have to remain at school. He is too far from home (1), he will probably not be able to find a friend whose family will react differently (3). Option (4) is impossible. There is no basis to suppose that Option (5) is a possibility.

23. **(3) He does not recognize Odili's name.** (Analysis) The man's behavior indicates that he found out or remembered further information when he left the home. Option (1) is incorrect, since no suspicions were announced. Options (2), (4), and (5) have no support in the excerpt.

24. **(2) poor** (Analysis) The narrator uses the words "eke out" and "abuse" in reference to her sister's playing. Options (1) and (3) have no support. Options (4) and (5) cannot be inferred.

25. **(3) The narrator is more secretive than Mona.** (Comparison/Contrast—Analysis) The narrator is covering up for her mother in some way. The other options may be true, but cannot be inferred from the excerpt.

26. **(4) Eugenie** (Analysis) Eugenie must expect the umbrella to be returned to her, according to lines 31–32. The other options are thus incorrect.

27. **(5) have recently immigrated** (Analysis) The reference to "Americans" suggests strongly a mother who feels part of a different culture. Options (1) and (3) may be true, but are not relevant. Options (2) and (4) are false.

28. **(2) victim** (Comprehension) This information is stated in the excerpt. There is no evidence for options (1) or (5). Photographs (option 3) are mentioned in the excerpt, but no photographers. The only police officer (option 4) whose name is given is Marti.

29. **(2) The police want Joe to identify some people who have been killed.** (Analysis) Marti doesn't actually say why she is showing Joe the pictures, but it becomes clear that this is the reason. Options (1) and (3) are incorrect because the police are not interested in how Joe sells or gives away food. Option (4) is incorrect because Joe is not trying to keep anyone away. There is no photographer in the story, so option (5) is incorrect.

30. **(1) He tried to help them.** (Analysis) Joe describes how he left food out for the "old ones" to take, so he was clearly trying to help. There is no support for any of the other options.

31. **(3) confining and harsh** (Analysis) The narrator's description of military school is summed up in one sentence that starts in line 3: "And so follows a miserable succession of bugle-blowing prisons, grim reveille-ridden summer camps." From this, none of the other choices reflects how he feels.

32. **(2) slightly chilly** (Analysis) "Fruitcake weather" is a "coming of winter morning," so options (1), (3), (4), and (5) would not apply.

33. **(1) was depressed** (Synthesis) The changes in her behavior are indications of depression. She did not find a new friend (option 2) or get a new pet (option 5). She was always somewhat superstitious (option 3), and she didn't start a bakery (option 4).

34. **(5) Part of him feels lost.** (Comprehension) There is no evidence for options (1), (2), (3), or (4) in the passage. His reaction to the death of his friend as "severing from me an irreplaceable part of myself, letting it loose like a kite on a broken string" and his looking "for a lost pair of kites" indicate that (5) is the only logical answer.

35. **(1) His family won't let him.** (Comprehension) It is clear that Buddy hates military school and that he has a new home that he doesn't really like, so option (4) and option (5) are wrong. He considers the home that he loves to be the place where his friend is, so option (2) is incorrect. His friend never told him to leave, so option (3) is wrong. It was "Those who Know Best" who made the decision, so we can infer that they are, in fact, members of his family.

UNIT 3: Poetry
(pages 44–53)

1. **(3) She lived an active, happy life.** (Synthesis) All the details in the poem show Lucinda engaged actively in a life she loved. Options (1) and (2) are true but too limited to describe her life. Option (4) is not supported by the excerpt. Option (5) is contradicted by the poem.

2. **(4) later generations** (Analysis) These lines seem to refer to young people of a later time. Although the reference could be to her own sons and daughters (option 1) or to other children (option 2), there is no evidence in the poem to suggest she was disappointed in them specifically. Options (3) and (5) do not make sense since the reference is to "sons and daughters."

3. **(1) She had an inner joy.** (Synthesis) This line and others in the poem show Lucinda's joyous approach to life. Options (2) and (3) are contradicted by the text. Options (4) and (5) are not supported by the text.

4. **(5) Work hard, but enjoy life.** (Application) Lucinda's life illustrates this philosophy. All the other options express ideas that are contrary to Lucinda's beliefs.

5. **(5) It is sad.** (Comprehension) The strain is melancholy. All other options are untrue or cannot be inferred.

6. **(3) The speaker shifts the focus to himself.** (Analysis) The last stanza is the only one in which the speaker uses the pronoun "I" and writes about himself. Options (1) and (2) are contradicted in the poem. Option (4) is incorrect because the poet refers to his feelings about the scene with the girl singing. Option (5) is not supported by the poem.

7. **(4) This experience will remain in his memory.** (Analysis) The speaker says the music remained with him for a long time. Therefore, all the other options are incorrect.

8. **(5) the funeral** (Comprehension) The reference to the "dark parade," the funeral, is in the future tense. All of the other options are expressed in the present, as if being seen by the speaker.

9. **(2) mechanically** (Analysis) This word suggests that the people in the house are not acting in a normal way, that their emotions are temporarily on "automatic pilot." Options (1) and (3) do not have this connotation. The other options suggest distaste (option 4) or mystery (option 5), not numbness.

10. **(4) activities of the living** (Synthesis) Horror (option 2) and distress (option 5) are not part of this poem. The observer shows no reaction (option 3), but simply says what he sees. The people described are not necessarily mourning (option 1); rather they are doing the things that must be done to bury the dead and go on with living.

11. **(4) to suggest that death is mysterious and alien to children** (Analysis) The key is in the use of pronouns. It shows how the children cannot see the dead as a person. That also underlines a distance between the children and an understanding of death. Option (1) is not true. Options (2) and (5) are not as important to the children as the strangeness of death itself. Option (3) is wrong because the phrase refers to their curiosity, not their fear.

12. **(2) man living across the street** (Analysis) Lines 1–2 refer to "the opposite house," and line 13 refers to when the speaker was a boy. Therefore, the other options are incorrect.

13. **(4) undertaker** (Analysis) Many people fear death and find the funeral business associated with it "appalling." Options (1) and (2) are incorrect because these occupations have nothing to do with death. The minister (option 3) and the doctor (option 5) are mentioned in the poem but not in the verse that refers to the "appalling trade."

14. **(3) to suggest that there are two speakers** (Synthesis) The speaker in quotation marks is asking questions, not being quoted (option 2). The unmarked stanzas are replies by another speaker to those questions, eliminating options (1) and (4). Option (5) is wrong because all stanzas are dialogue, not description.

15. **(2) It is an imaginary conversation.** (Synthesis) The poem is spoken between two people; therefore, it is a conversation. One of the people is dead, so it is imaginary. Option (1) is too general and not truly accurate. The remaining options are false.

16. **(5) He is dead.** (Synthesis) Line 4 provides the first clue and is reinforced throughout the poem. Sleep (line 24) for this speaker is only figurative (option 1). There is no support for options (2), (3), or (4).

17. **(3) Life continues even after an individual dies.** (Synthesis) The friend in this poem has not betrayed the dead man (option 1), nor has the woman (option 2). They have simply gone on with life. The poet is not necessarily suggesting that ghosts exist (option 4) or that he believes in the immortality of the soul (option 5); having the dead man ask questions is a device by which to explore the central question.

18. **(3) They each found something.** (Comprehension) Although their discoveries were different, each girl found something on the beach. Options (1), (2), and (4) are not suggested by the poem. Although option (5) might apply to three of the girls, it probably wasn't true of molly, who didn't enjoy what she found.

19. **(4) molly was more easily scared than the others.** (Analysis) While the other discoveries seem somewhat magical, molly's seems frightening. But what the poet describes is a crab, not really a horrible thing. What makes it horrible is molly's own fear, the self she found in the sea. Options (1) and (3) are contradicted by evidence in the poem. There is no support for options (2) and (5).

20. **(2) It emphasizes the break between the story and the poet.** (Synthesis) A poet's use of an unusual feature often indicates emphasis; in this case, it emphasizes the transition between description and analysis. Option (1) is wrong because the other complete sentence is not capitalized. There is no support for options (3) or (5). Option (4) is wrong because there is no change in rhythm.

21. **(4) to suggest the mysterious quality may saw in the stone** (Analysis) The two comparisons help the reader see the stone as unusual because we do not normally call a world small or think of the word alone in terms of size. Option (1) is wrong because the description is figurative, not realistic. There is no relation between the similes and the suggestions in options (2) and (3). Option (5) is wrong because, although the shell also has a mysterious quality, the similes do not compare the two objects.

22. **(5) It gives the poem a pleasing repetition of sounds.** (Analysis) Alliteration, the repetition of initial consonant sounds, is a common poetic device that can provide a pleasing effect. Option (1) is untrue. Option (2) might be true but is not significant to understanding or enjoying the poem. There is no support for option (3). Option (4) is incorrect because monotony is not a quality the poet would want in this poem.

23. **(4) a man writing to his newborn granddaughter** (Analysis) Options (1) and (3) are wrong because the speaker in the poem wrote these words (line 18), rather than spoke them. Although we are given no clue as to the speaker's gender, we do know the child's name is Emily (the poem's title), that she might grow up to be a mother (line 15), and that she is "two generations away" (line 2), making the speaker a grandparent, so options (2) and (5) are wrong.

24. **(2) fifty-three** (Comprehension) This information is stated in line 3. Option (1) refers to the child's future, and options (3) and (4) refer to the speaker's future.

25. **(3) Love endures.** (Synthesis) Options (1) and (5) may be true, but they are not suggested in the poem. Option (2) is suggested in the poem but only as an example of the main idea. Option (4) is too limited to summarize the speaker's message. Option (3) is supported by the poet's emphasis on love and is essentially a paraphrase of lines 15 and 16.

26. **(3) to know about this poem** (Comprehension) In line 13 the speaker says that Emily will have read her children the poem. Option (1) is incorrect because it is the opposite of what the speaker says in line 12. Option (2) is contradicted by the poem. There is no evidence in the poem for options (4) or (5).

27. **(4) a street address** (Analysis) A street address can appear on a front gate, and that is the best explanation for the reference here. There is no evidence in the poem for options (1), (2), and (3). Option (5) is incorrect because a ZIP code would not logically be on a gate.

28. **(2) her nose** (Comprehension) This information is stated in the poem (lines 20–21). All the other items were painted, but not because of an itch; therefore, they are incorrect.

29. **(4) the posts** (Analysis) All the other options are things that would not normally be painted, even option (3), which she explains in line 13.

30. **(3) lighthearted** (Analysis) There is no support for options (1) or (2). Option (4) is too strong a word. Option (5) is not accurate because the speaker is laughing at herself.

31. **(3) Blue is associated with the post office.** (Analysis) There is no real support for the other options, but the post office, which uses mailboxes, is associated with the color blue. Option (5) is clearly wrong given the speaker's happy mood.

32. **(2) make enough for ten people** (Application) The speaker tends to get carried away and do things in excess. Options (1), (3), and (5) suggest more discipline than the speaker seems to have. There is no support for option (4).

33. **(4) His work required hard labor.** (Analysis) Option (1) is incorrect because of the <u>too</u> in line 1. Options (2) and (3) are contradicted by lines 3 and 4. Option (5) has no support in the poem.

34. **(3) warmth and cold** (Analysis) Although all options are mentioned in the poem, the repeated images of warmth and cold emphasize the warmth of the father's love contrasted with the son's cold indifference.

35. **(2) the father's dutiful care of the family** (Analysis) The simple but lonely task of lighting the fires was done out of love. Options (1) and (5) refer to the son, but he was not the one who loved. Option (3) refers to an opposite emotional climate. Option (4) is wrong, being based on necessity, not love.

36. **(4) He regrets his thoughtless lack of understanding.** (Synthesis) The last two lines of the poem suggest that the poet has finally come to understand the value of his father's love. Options (1), (2), and (3) are the opposite of this, and option (5) has no support.

37. **(2) the fire was warming the rooms** (Analysis) Since line 7 says "when the rooms were warm," it makes sense to conclude that line 6 is figurative language describing the effect of the fire warming the cold rooms. Nothing in the poem supports any of the other options.

38. **(1) The boy would go to church.** (Analysis) The references in the poem to "Sundays" (line 1) and "polished my good shoes" (line 12) lead to the inference that the boy would be going to church. Options (2) and (3) are incorrect because there is no school or work on Sunday. Option (4) is not likely because this is not something we would expect this father to do. Option (5) is incorrect because "offices" in the last line doesn't refer to a place.

39. **(2) the envy of the angels** (Analysis) The repetition of the angelic imagery is a clue to its importance. The speaker believes that even heaven was aware of the beauty of their love. Love is not made special by age (option 1), by death (option 3), by the cause of death (option 5), or by status (option 4).

40. **(4) continue to mourn his lost love** (Application) The speaker's moody reflection on Annabel Lee shows no sign of ending soon; therefore, option (1) is wrong. The speaker is estranged from her family (option 5), but option (2) is too extreme a reaction. The speaker actually resents the angel's interference, so option (3) is unlikely.

41. **(3) become the speaker's devoted wife** (Application) Annabel Lee's only thought was to love and be loved by the speaker. There is no evidence to suggest options (1) or (5). Options (2) and (4) are not supported in the poem.

42. (4) repeating "a kingdom by the sea" (Analysis) Pay attention to repetition. This phrase occurs frequently and suggests mystery and romance because it reminds the reader of fairy tales without being specific. Although option (1) may contribute to the overall mood, it is secondary to the repetition. Options (2) and (3) do not create mood. Option (5) is wrong because we know the death was caused by a chill.

43. (5) still loves Annabel Lee. (Synthesis) He speaks with passion about what happened many years ago. Apparently he is still obsessed with recalling the love they shared. There is no support for options (1), (2), (3), or (4).

44. (3) an elaborate tomb (Comprehension) A noble person would have an elaborate final resting place. Options (1) and (4) are wrong because they suggest she is alive. Options (2) and (5) are wrong because of the phrase "shut up."

45. (3) the narrator's passion (Expanded Synthesis) In the quote, Poe promises to "worship beauty." In the poem, the narrator describes his powerful love for the "beautiful Annabel Lee." The remaining options are either irrelevant to the quote or untrue.

46. (3) a fall evening (Comprehension) This information is in line 6. There is no support for the other options.

47. (1) threatening (Comprehension) Most of what is described in the first ten lines is threatening, i.e., the threat of a storm. Ugly (option 2) is similar but less precise. Options (3), (4), and (5) would better apply to the speaker's reactions than to the tone.

48. (1) deprived of a loved one by death (Analysis) The tone of the poem is somber and very sad, and the speaker describes a state of being completely alone except for God. Option (1) is the only option that accounts for these factors. All the others do not explain this great aloneness.

UNIT 4: Drama
(pages 54–63)

1. **(2) a rich man's house** (Synthesis) Support can be found in that servants can be hired, Johansson has wanted to see the house (homes of the rich are generally appealing), and dinner parties are a regular affair. Option (1) refers to Bengtsson's simile in line 25, not reality. The same is true of the ghost metaphor (option 3). There is no evidence for options (4) or (5).

2. **(4) unusual conversation between people** (Application) Option (1) is eliminated by Bengtsson's description in lines 19–24. Options (2) and (5) are unlikely, considering how peculiar the people sound. Option (3) is incorrect because it is based only on a metaphor.

3. **(5) to provide further information about the household** (Analysis) Information about the household is provided as a result of Johansson's questioning. Option (1) is a fact, not a reason. There is no support for the other options.

4. **(2) never worked in this house before** (Analysis) Johansson has dreamed of working in this house (lines 11–12), but since this is his first evening there he must ask questions about the event. Therefore, options (1), (3), and (5) are incorrect. Option (4) is incorrect because, although he does think the people are peculiar, this doesn't keep him from wanting to work there.

5. **(4) knows Johansson slightly** (Synthesis) Two reasons make this option the best choice: Johansson uses the phrase "as you know" (Line 9), and Bengtsson is very willing to tell Johansson about the eccentricities of the household. Therefore, all the other options are incorrect.

6. **(4) implies that she alone knows what is best for Barbara** (Synthesis) Lady Britomart's belief that she alone knows what is best for people is supported throughout the excerpt. Although she might be concerned about Barbara's welfare (option 2), she doesn't show any faith in anyone else's opinion (option 3). There is no support for options (1) and (5).

7. **(4) showing that he is wary of her interference** (Analysis) Stephen is wary of his mother's interfering in his personal life, though he tries to hide this behind a polite exterior. Options (1), (2), (3), and (5) are not supported by the evidence.

8. **(1) He is simple, quiet, and refined.** (Analysis) This answer is the only option that is deemed positive and not deemed negative by one or the other of the speakers. Options (2) and (3) are untrue of Cusins. Option (4) cannot be inferred. Option (5) is seen as negative.

9. **(5) amusement** (Synthesis) While both characters in this excerpt probably take themselves seriously, the audience will find their discussion rather funny, especially Lady Britomart's inability to see her own snobbishness. Options (1), (2), (3), and (4) would be the results of misunderstanding the play.

10. **(3) write about everything except the assigned topic** (Application) Helena does tend to ignore the other person's remarks and tends to ramble from subject to subject. She takes herself seriously (option 4) and cannot be described as either clear (option 1), timid (option 2), or logical (option 5).

11. **(4) The Ignored Suitor** (Application) Helena ignores Voitski's remarks except when they begin to annoy her. She is not really concerned about her husband (option 3) or the environment (option 2). There is no support for options (1) and (5).

12. **(2) as a melodramatic person** (Analysis) Voitski's dialogue could be interpreted as melodramatic, as material straight from a soap opera. Options (3) and (5) imply more maturity and control than Voitski exhibits. He is not purposely being jolly (option 1) or rude (option 4).

13. **(4) statement that men have no mercy** (Analysis) There is not enough support for options (1), (2), or (3). Option (5) is opposite to Helena's belief.

14. **(1) Helena and Voitski** (Comprehension) This information is given in lines 32–34 where Helena addresses Voitski by Ivan, his first name. Therefore, all the other options are incorrect.

15. **(4) church parish** (Synthesis) Fitzgibbon's later discussion of a church parish suggests that St. Dominic's is similar. There is no evidence for the other options.

16. **(1) software troubleshooter** (Application) O'Malley's job seems to be to fix things that have gone wrong, not to be a planner or a promoter as suggested by the other options.

17. **(1) show how well these men know each other** (Analysis) The directions indicate emotions or actions that demonstrate concern and assurance. None of the other options have support in the stage directions.

18. **(2) He is actually describing his own earlier behavior.** (Analysis) Options (1), (4), and (5) are not suggested by innocently. Option (3) is wrong because the rest of the text does not support that the Father is unaware of (innocent of) how much like the other old priest he is.

19. **(4) hearing about his brother's success** (Analysis) Willy is responding to his brother's declaration, "I was rich." Option (1) is attractive, but not accurate in the context. Options (2) and (3) cannot be inferred from the context. Option (5) cannot be inferred from the excerpt.

20. **(5) Ben is older than Willy.** (Analysis) Willy's memories of childhood indicate that he was the younger child. Option (1) cannot be inferred. Options (2), (3), and (4) are incorrect.

21. **(1) how he succeeded** (Synthesis). The answer to Willy's question comes in the text of the excerpt. Options (2) and (5) are attractive responses, but do not fit the emphasis on success. Options (3) and (4) cannot be inferred.

22. **(1) never got in touch with him** (Analysis) It is clear from the passage that Ben has not seen Willy since he was three years old, and it would be natural for Willy to wonder why Ben didn't get in touch. Lines 16–17 show that Willy knew Ben had gone to look for their father, so he wouldn't have wondered why Ben left. There is no support for any of the other options.

23. **(2) disapproving** (Analysis) Amanda's tone is a bit caustic. The other options cannot be inferred from the immediate context of the quote.

24. **(1) to meet Laura** (Analysis) This answer can be inferred from Amanda's response to Tom in lines 52–53. The other options either cannot be inferred in the context of the quote or are contradicted elsewhere in the excerpt.

25. **(3) dangerous** (Analysis) This answer can be understood from the remainder of the sentence: "No girl can do worse…" The other options either cannot be inferred from the context or are incorrect.

26. **(1) more supportive** (Comparison/Contrast—Analysis) This answer can be inferred from Margaret's defense of Gene in lines 45–46. Option (4) cannot be inferred, since Tom's aggressive quarreling does not automatically imply a lack of interest in his son. The remaining options are incorrect.

27. **(2) is conniving** (Analysis) This answer correctly analyzes the subtext of the stage directions and Tom's words in lines 26–30. Option (1) has no basis for support. Options (4) and (5) take the words of the stage directions too literally. Option (3) is incorrect.

28. **(3) He feels defensive about his age.** (Synthesis) This answer can be inferred from the allusions to memory and the suggestion that Tom too fondly remembers his past. The remaining options either cannot be inferred from the excerpt or are irrelevant to the question.

29. **(4) Tom is quarreling with Gene.** (Comprehension) Margaret's words indicate her support of Gene, whether he is right about the drive or wrong. She is reacting to Tom's refusal to accept Gene's decision. Options (2), (3) and (5) cannot be inferred from the excerpt. Option (1) is irrelevant to Margaret.

30. **(2) have not seen each other in years** (Analysis) Although never stated directly, it's clear from the conversation that the two women have known each other for many years. Therefore, options (1), (3), and (4) are incorrect. Option (5) is incorrect because both women seem to be enjoying the conversation.

31. **(3) She thinks Gina looks foolish.** (Synthesis) Maggy ridicules Gina's appearance on the float. Therefore, option (1) is incorrect. Option (2) is incorrect because Maggy doesn't seem to have a high opinion of Robbie Bigelow. Options (4) and (5) are incorrect because they are contrary to what is stated or implied in the conversation.

32. **(4) talks a lot** (Application) Based on her behavior in this situation, it is reasonable to assume that Maggy will be talkative in other similar situations. Options (1), (2), and (3) seem unlikely based on the excerpt. Option (5) is incorrect because Maggy seems to enjoy conversations with friends.

33. **(2) He doesn't believe he is a very good teacher.** (Comprehension) There is no real evidence for options (1), (3), (4), or (5). Frank does, however, say that he is an appalling teacher and repeats this idea throughout the passage.

34. **(4) You can't make a silk purse out of a sow's ear.** (Application) Frank believes that he could not be as good an instructor as Rita needs, even if he tried. He is the sow's ear and what Rita needs is the silk purse. The other options all refer to the use of time, not skill.

35. **(2) It indicates that Rita has changed her mind.** (Analysis) The contrast in Rita's attitudes suggests a decision and change in mood. There is no support for options (1), (3), (4), and (5).

36. **(1) uncertainty** (Analysis) All four of the other options appear, but only briefly, in Frank's speech. He has doubts about himself and how to present himself. He hesitates and changes the subject often.

37. **(4) He thinks he knows absolutely nothing.** (Comprehension). This information is stated in lines 20–22. Options (1) and (2) are contradicted by the excerpt. Option (3) is true, but is a reason he gives for being a good teacher. Option (5) is not a reason he is a terrible teacher.

38. **(4) He was assigned as her tutor.** (Comprehension) Rita says she wants him as her teacher because he was assigned to her and she doesn't want anyone else. Options (1) and (5) are not supported by the excerpt. Options (2) and (3) are not true.

39. **(3) to attract the men's attention** (Comprehension) Coughing is a way to attract attention, and that is what these women want. There is no support for options (1), (2), or (5). Option (4) is incorrect because the men are apparently not looking at them.

40. **(4) demonstrate how casual they are** (Comprehension) Although the whistling might annoy the women, the more important interpretation is that the men appear to be relaxed and unconcerned with whatever is bothering the women. There is no support for the other options.

41. **(5) make the audience laugh** (Analysis) This is a silly remark (option 1), and it bears no relation to repentance (option 2). Eating muffins has little to do with sensitivity (option 3) or the time of day (option 4). That anyone could see eating muffins as a sign of repentance is funny.

42. **(3) Gwendolen will be the first to speak.** (Application) These women are neither as dignified nor as aloof as they would like to pretend. As they very much want the men's company, Gwendolen will probably "break the ice" that the men aren't even aware of. Options (1) and (5) are not in accord with the women's characters. Option (2) is wrong because it disregards the men's casual attitude. Option (4) is unlikely.

43. **(1) English upper class** (Comprehension) The group speaks in formal language which one would suspect of that social level. There is no support for option (2). The one song does not suggest option (3), nor do the muffins suggest option (4). There is no evidence for option (5).

SIMULATED TEST A

(pages 64–74)

1. **(2) too excited to sleep** (Comprehension) This information is given in the text. Therefore, options (1), (4), and (5) are incorrect. The mother, not Turtle, is interested in the man's bald spot (option 3).

2. **(5) a character in a pirate story** (Synthesis) This information is not stated directly but can be inferred from Taylor's use of the words "pirate" and "Captain Hook" as she thinks about Turtle's question. Option (1) is incorrect because the captain introduces himself as only "your captain." Jax (option 2) is mentioned, but his last name is not given. There is no name given for the man in the next seat (option 3). There is no mention of Turtle's father (option 4).

3. **(3) They have probably flown before.** (Analysis) This inference can be made from the statement that "Everybody else on the plane is behaving as though they are simply sitting in chairs a little too close together" (lines 51–53). There is no information to support any of the other options.

4. **(1) They often do things without thinking of the consequences.** (Synthesis) Moving through the water headfirst, as with moving through the world headfirst, would mean that one's eyes were not fixed on where he or she was going—not "seeing" or thinking of the consequences. Options (2), (4), and (5) have no support in the excerpt. Option (3) is unlikely.

5. **(3) cluttered** (Analysis) References to stacks of newspapers, wrappers, and Jessie's searching through cabinets provide this information. There is no support for the other options.

6. **(2) She would give Jessie only some of her attention.** (Application) Jessie and Mama don't seem to communicate on the same "wave length," especially at the beginning of the excerpt. Option (1) is the opposite of how Mama acts in this scene. There is no support for options (3), (4), or (5).

7. **(5) to make the audience wonder what Jessie is planning to do** (Analysis) The collection of items is odd enough to suggest that Jessie is planning something unusual. Options (1) and (2) have no support. Option (3) is incorrect because Jessie shows little concern about Saturday night. Option (4) is denied by Jessie.

8. **(3) having them carry on what are almost two separate conversations** (Analysis) The two women do seem to be talking about different subjects, indicating that there is an emotional distance between them. Although they don't ignore each other, they also don't really pay attention. No support is given for options (1) or (2). Option (4) reveals something about Mama only. Option (5) is wrong because neither expresses any emotion.

9. **(4) redo her fingernail polish** (Comprehension) Mama refers to her chipped fingernails; Jessie admits that doing Mama's nails is on the schedule. There is no support for the other options.

10. **(2) is fairly lazy** (Synthesis) Mama does not pick up the dessert wrapper or do her own nails. She also just took a nap. There is no support for options (1), (3), or (4). Option (5) is wrong because she nags Jessie.

11. **(5) the last line of the poem** (Analysis) The phrase is the beginning of an explanation of how the speaker can let go. Options (1) and (2) bear no relation to the phrase. The poet is trying to convey a much different idea than those in options (3) and (4).

12. **(4) loving regret** (Synthesis) The speaker is anticipating the loss of her beloved, but all the while is continuing to love. Options (1), (2), (3), and (5) suggest emotions not expressed in the poem.

13. **(3) understanding in human relationships** (Application) All the other options deal with generalities. The poet appears to be more concerned with the nature of the individual.

14. **(4) She's thinking about how other lovers will see these things.** (Analysis) There is no evidence for options (1) or (5). Option (3) is wrong because of the complexity of the descriptions. Option (2) would lessen the impact of the poem.

15. **(2) brown** (Comprehension) Copper pennies in dark honey are brown. There is no evidence for the other options.

16. **(5) preparing herself to be alone** (Synthesis) In recognizing that she cannot stop the person from leaving and in accepting the fact, she is preparing herself. There is no evidence for options (1), (2), or (4). The speaker is somewhat selfish in that she is letting go slowly, so option (3) is wrong.

17. **(2) to notify the member of loan terms** (Synthesis) This option is sufficiently broad to cover the letter content. The remaining options are too narrow.

18. **(4) assessment of a late fee** (Analysis) This option is alluded to in the letter. None of the other options are mentioned. Options (1) and (2) would be too severe for one month's tardiness. Option (3) is implausible. Option (5) cannot be inferred.

19. **(2) Payments will automatically be transferred from the member's Credit Union account.** (Comprehension) This is the only option that is stated in the passage.

20. **(2) the repayment provisions** (Expanded Synthesis) The brochure notes advantages unavailable at commercial banks. The repayment provisions are explicitly more advantageous at the Credit Union than at commercial banks. The remaining options are essentially similar to those at commercial banks or cannot be inferred.

21. **(5) Repayment Method form letter** (Comprehension) This option is directly stated in lines 10–12. The other options do not correspond with the abbreviation following "encl."

22. **(2) Interest on loans helps pay for member benefits.** (Analysis) This option connects the loan to the benefits of other members. Options (3) and (4) focus on benefits for the loan recipient. Options (1) and (5) are untrue.

23. **(3) that Minta really had forgotten Brownie** (Synthesis) Earlier Minta had imagined herself saying she would never forget to feed Brownie, but she did forget. Although options (2) and (5) may be true, they are not important here. There is no evidence for options (1) or (4).

24. **(3) It shows that Minta is imagining what she will tell her parents.** (Analysis) The italics indicate what is going through Minta's mind. Option (1) is about the past, not the future. There is no support for options (2), (4), or (5).

25. **(4) a stabbing knife** (Comprehension) Minta imagines being stabbed after the door is broken in. Options (1) and (2) do not fit thrusting steel. The description would be odd for option (3) and an awkward metaphor for option (5).

26. **(3) Mrs. Beal** (Comprehension) It is Mrs. Beal at the door. Only in Minta's imagination are options (1) and (2) possible. Option (4) is wrong because the daughter is probably at home. There is no evidence for option (5).

27. **(3) She is no longer afraid to be alone in the house.** (Synthesis) Minta is brought back to warm reality and is no longer afraid; therefore, options (4) and (5) are wrong. There is no evidence for options (1) and (2).

28. **(2) sympathetically** (Application) This option is clearly supported by the tone and content of the selection. Options (1), (3), and (4) are negative—unlikely, given the author's concerns. Option (5) is attractive, but cannot be inferred from the selection.

29. **(3) sad** (Synthesis) This option is reflected in the tone and content of the selection. Options (1) and (2) have slightly negative connotations, given the subject matter. Option (4) suggests excessive positive emotion. Option (5) does not fit with the author's passionate approach.

30. **(1) ethnic food** (Analysis) The allusion to spice is intended to contrast many foods from different lands to the relatively bland American-style food. Option (4) is too limited. Options (2), (3), and (5) relate to American-style food.

31. **(3) The children don't share their grandparents' language and culture.** (Analysis) This option explains the allusion to a "memory of exile" and explains the inarticulateness of children both in terms of language and cultural aspects. The remaining options either cannot be inferred or are irrelevant.

32. **(2) His parents were immigrants.** (Synthesis) This option can be inferred from the entire passage. Lines 14–15 tell us that the author is American born. His sympathy with the children of immigrants suggests that he is one. The remaining options are either unlikely or untrue.

33. **(2) He enjoys the airiness.** (Synthesis—Comparison/Contrast) This option expresses the husband's only stated preference. The other options either cannot be inferred or are untrue.

34. **(3) She is artistically inclined.** (Analysis) This option accounts for her critique of the paper design. Option (1) may be true, but is not the best answer. Options (2), (4), and (5) either cannot be inferred or are too vague.

35. **(1) is unhappy** (Analysis) The room, her depiction of John's patronizing care, and having to write in secret, all seem to point to her unhappiness. Option (2) is wrong; she found plenty to write about. Option (3) is not a result of John's "prescriptions." Options (4) and (5) are not supported by the excerpt.

36. **(2) evokes our sense of smell** (Analysis) The word "sulfur" reminds us not only of color, but of stifling odor, as well. The purpose of the image is to convey the narrator's negative sense of the room. The remaining options are either irrelevant or positive.

37. **(1) story takes place in the country** (Analysis) The allusion to nature suggests a country setting. Option (2) is possible, but not in accordance with a garden setting. The remaining options cannot be inferred.

38. **(1) He is worried that writing will tax her too much.** (Expanded Synthesis) It is clear from the passage that the narrator is viewed as ill by her husband. Since she is forbidden to work, the only evidence we have of her work is her writing. There is no specific evidence for option (2). The remaining options cannot be inferred.

39. **(3) psychotherapy** (Application) The narrator seems to be suffering from an emotional or psychological condition, not a physical ailment. Her husband thinks he's taking good care of her, but she feels stifled by him. Options (1), (2), (4), and (5) are all medical treatments not supported by information in the passage.

40. **(1) respectful** (Synthesis) This option is the best choice, given the narrator's careful allusions to her husband's power over her life choices. Options (2), (3), and (4) have no support in the excerpt. Option (5) seems unlikely, given the implied frailty of the narrator.

SIMULATED TEST B

(pages 76–86)

1. **(2) He's respected.** (Analysis) This answer can be inferred by analyzing both the audience reaction and the poet's reaction, both of which suggest respectability. Options (3) and (5) are not supported by the evidence. Option (1) suggests an entertaining, rather than a dry, pedantic lecturer. Option (4) may be true, but the applause is directed at the great lecturer.

2. **(1) understands the stars differently from the astronomer** (Analysis) The speaker understands the stars by experiencing them rather than by reducing them to charts and diagrams. He is not recovering from an illness (option 4), but feels "tired and sick" (lines 10–11) when he hears the lecture. None of the other options is supported by the poem.

3. **(5) bird-watching** (Application) Only this answer suggests communing with nature and a solitary endeavor. All of the other options are either contrary to the evidence or cannot be inferred.

4. **(1) distances from the sun** (Comprehension) Only this answer matches the context, which stresses dry, mathematical formulas, as opposed to imaginative figuration. Option (2) is plausible, but not as focused on numbers as the first. In addition, the figures are "ranged in columns." The remaining options cannot be inferred.

5. **(3) does not need to speak** (Analysis) This answer correctly responds to the underlying connection between poet and nature. The other options are unsupported by the evidence in the poem.

6. **(1) wants to experience nature, not hear about it** (Synthesis) The underlying message of the poem is best summarized in this answer. The remaining options are either wrong (options 3, 4, and 5) or irrelevant (option 2).

7. **(1) to summarize the plan provisions** (Synthesis) This answer best enunciates the purpose of the plan. Option (2) is too limited. Options (3), (4), and (5) are irrelevant or unsupported.

8. **(4) Flexible spending contributions will be after-tax contributions.** (Expanded Synthesis) This answer correctly matches information from the Plan Document with the summary of COBRA benefits. The remaining options are untrue.

9. **(3) Over-the-counter remedies are not defined as eligible.** (Application) This answer correctly identifies a requirement of the FSA as noted in lines 24–26. The remaining options are either contrary to common sense or cannot be inferred from the evidence.

10. **(1) They are not taxed.** (Analysis) The first two paragraphs set out provisions for contributions. Only option (1) is true.

11. **(4) employees** (Synthesis) The tone, language, and layout of the document indicate that the writers had in mind a non-expert audience. The remaining options are either too limited or too professional.

12. **(4) in an outdoors location** (Comprehension) The sketch was done in the backyard, eliminating options (1) and (3). Crane also states he doesn't use photographs (option 5). There is no support for option (2).

13. **(4) "Backyards are like portraits."** (Analysis) Crane feels that backyards reflect their owners' personalities. The other options do not allude to the human presence in landscapes.

14. **(3) immediately providing the reader with descriptive images** (Analysis) Option (3) steers the reader back to the text where multiple examples are given. Options (1), (2), (4), and (5) are only factors that are best summed up by the examples.

15. **(1) linking her conclusion to her introduction** (Synthesis) These words refer back to her phrase "seethe with life of the moment" and so give unity to the paragraph. She enjoys the vigor of the paintings, so option (2) is incorrect. Option (3) refers to what Crane says. Option (4) is incorrect because she is expressing her own opinion. Option (5) has no support.

16. **(2) alive** (Comprehension) The reviewer is referring to the liveliness and sense of humanity. There is no support for the other options.

17. **(5) mutiny** (Synthesis) It can be inferred from the details in the excerpt that crew members have taken over a ship. Therefore, all the other options are incorrect.

18. **(2) two guns** (Comprehension) This detail is given in lines 12–13. Option (1) is incorrect because it was the curtain that was blue and no mention is made of a shirt. The excerpt says specifically that the captain was not found (option 3). Option (4) is incorrect because they found one hat. The fireman in option (5) refers to a member of the ship's crew who was not in the cabin.

19. **(1) Peter** (Synthesis) The action in the excerpt shows that Peter was in charge. Options (2), (3), and (4) are incorrect because all of these characters defer to Peter. Option (5) is incorrect because, while the captain might once have been in charge, he is missing.

20. **(3) bully** (Synthesis) Turno not only beats up Aaron, but taunts him as well. Therefore, he is not a weakling (option 1) or a prankster (option 2). There is no evidence for options (4) or (5).

21. **(3) agreeing to dance with her** (Comprehension) This refers to Eugene's need to count as he dances. There is no evidence to support the other options.

22. **(4) in the army** (Synthesis) Eugene's learning to march and having to do push-ups both suggest this. Option (1) is wrong because he is clearly not much of a dancer. Option (2) is wrong because having the same first name as an author does not make him one. There is no evidence for options (3) or (5).

23. **(2) to show how Daisy and Eugene are supposed to move** (Comprehension) Most of the directions refer to where the two are putting their hands and feet. Options (1) and (3) have no support. Option (4) is wrong because the directions are simple. Option (5) is wrong because the dialogue alone is not enough to suggest what is happening.

24. **(3) it is a way to start a conversation** (Synthesis) Daisy and Eugene have just met and are getting acquainted. Options (1) and (2) may be true, but neither is the reason for the long talk. Option (4) does not explain why they talk about their names. Option (5) is not true.

25. **(2) laugh at the couple** (Analysis) The dialogue is slightly silly and amusing. Option (1) is wrong because Daisy is doing fine. A vague coincidence of names is not enough to justify option (3). What is happening is not exciting enough to provoke options (4) or (5).

26. **(5) be friendly** (Application) The two are on fairly good terms here and probably will continue to be so. Nothing has occurred to embarrass either person (option 1), nor to justify an extreme emotional response as in options (2) and (3). There is no support for option (4).

27. **(1) teacher** (Application) Emma's desire to form and guide Harriet is the clue to this answer. The remaining options range from the vaguely possible to the improbable.

28. **(3) created a vacuum in Emma's life for Harriet to fill** (Analysis) This answer can be inferred by analyzing the passage on walking. The remaining options are either factually wrong or cannot be inferred.

29. **(4) the weather** (Analysis) This answer requires analysis of the words "as the year varied" (line 14). Option (1) cannot be inferred. Options (2), (3), and (5) are either illogical or unsupported by the evidence.

30. **(2) appreciation** (Application) The answer is evident from the analysis of Harriet's character. The remaining options are either negative (1), (3), and (4) or unlikely, given Harriet's station (5).

31. **(3) friends** (Analysis) The answer requires an analysis of the sentences from line 35 through 40. Options (1), (2), and (5) make no sense in the context. Option (4) has no basis in the grammar of the sentences in question.

32. **(2) no longer exercised properly** (Analysis) The answer requires analysis of lines 14–16. The remaining options can be discounted as either exaggerated—option (1)—or unsupported—options (3), (4), and (5).

33. **(1) is not as clever** (Synthesis—Comparison/Contrast) Harriet's intelligence is compared implicitly to Mrs. Weston in the disparagement of Harriet's understanding (lines 34–35) and the esteem Emma feels for Mrs. Weston. The remaining options can be discounted as either unsupported—(2) and (4)—or contrary to evidence—(3) and (5).

34. **(3) indicate that anyone like Harriet would do** (Analysis) This answer requires analysis of the phrase's grammar. The "a" is indefinite, suggesting that Harriet is a type. The remaining options are either unsupported by the grammar—(2) and (4)—or unclear as an answer—(1) and (5).

35. **(2) an electronic game machine** (Comprehension) Checker Charley is the name of the machine. Options (1), (3), (4), and (5) are wrong because they refer to people.

36. **(3) expects to lose the game** (Synthesis) Paul is comparing the likelihood of his winning to the sun not rising, but the sun always rises (option 1). Option (2) is the opposite of option (3). Options (4) and (5) are not true.

37. **(2) He believes he will win the money.** (Synthesis) There is no evidence for options (1), (3), or (4). Berringer would have no reason to signal Paul (option 5), but he does expect to take the money home.

38. **(5) Paul is ahead.** (Comprehension) Paul is taking the checker pieces. There is no evidence for the other options.

39. **(3) confident** (Synthesis) Lines 1–11 provide details that lead to this inference. Therefore, all the other options are incorrect.

40. **(2) extremely** (Synthesis) This meaning of the term best fits the context. Therefore, all the other options are incorrect.

Grateful acknowledgment is made to the following authors, agents, and publishers for permission to reprint copyrighted materials. Every effort has been made to trace ownership of all copyrighted material and to secure the necessary permissions to reprint. Any errors or omissions will be corrected in future printings.

Anderson, Robert. From *I Never Sang for My Father* by Robert Anderson. Reprinted by permission of the author. **(p. 60)**

Associated Press. Review of "'RedShift 4' Software Praised" by Larry Blasko. Reprinted with permission of The Associated Press. **(p. 11)**

James Baldwin Estate. Excerpted from "Sonny's Blues" by James Baldwin. Copyright © 1957, copyright renewed. Published in *Going to Meet the Man*, Vintage Books. Reprinted by arrangement with the James Baldwin Estate. **(p. 29)**

Georges Borchardt, Inc. "Does America Still Exist?" by Richard Rodriguez. Copyright © 1984 by Richard Rodriguez. Originally appeared in *Harper's*. Reprinted by permission of Georges Borchardt, Inc., for the author. **(p. 72)**

Butterfield, Catherine. From *Joined At The Head* by Catherine Butterfield. Copyright © 1993. Reprinted by permission of the author. **(p. 61)**

DaSilva, Gary. Excerpt from *Biloxi Blues* copyright © 1986 by Neil Simon. Reprinted by permission of the author. Professionals and amateurs are hereby warned that *Biloxi Blues* is fully protected under the Berne Convention and the Universal Copyright Convention and is subject to royalty. All rights, including without limitation professional, amateur, motion picture, television, radio, recitation, lecturing, public reading and foreign translation rights, computer media rights and the right of reproduction, and electronic storage or retrieval, in whole or in part and in any form, are strictly reserved and none of these rights can be exercised or used without written permission from the copyright owner. Inquiries for stock and amateur performances should be addressed to Samuel French, Inc., 45 West 25th Street, New York, NY 10010. All other inquiries should be addressed to Gary N. DaSilva, 111 N. Sepulveda Blvd., Suite 250, Manhattan Beach, CA 90266-6850. **(p. 82)**

Farrar, Straus and Giroux, LLC. From "The Jewbird" from *Idiots First* by Bernard Malamud. Copyright © 1963 by Bernard Malamud. Copyright renewed 1991 by Ann Malamud. Reprinted by permission of Farrar, Straus, and Giroux, LLC. **(p. 39)** Excerpt from *'Night Mother* by Marsha Norman. Copyright © 1983 by Marsha Norman. Reprinted by permission of Hill & Wang, a division of Farrar, Straus and Giroux, LLC. **(p. 66)**

Harcourt, Inc. Excerpt from "Flowering Judas" in *Flowering Judas and Other Stories*, copyright 1930 and renewed 1958 by Katherine Anne Porter. Reprinted by permission of Harcourt, Inc. **(p. 28)** From "Good Country People" from *A Good Man is Hard to Find and Other Stories*, copyright © 1955 by Flannery O'Connor and renewed 1983 by Regina O'Connor. Reprinted by permission of Harcourt, Inc. **(p. 30)** From "Twelve, Fall (A Child's Day)" from *Cress Delahanty* by Jessamyn West, copyright 1953 by Harcourt, Inc. and renewed 1981 by Jessamyn West, reprinted by permission of the publisher. **(p. 70)**

HarperCollins Publishers, Inc. From *Pigs in Heaven* by Barbara Kingsolver. Copyright © 1993 by Barbara Kingsolver. Reprinted by permission of HarperCollins Publishers, Inc. **(p. 65)**

Henry Holt and Company. "Bereft" by Robert Frost from *The Poetry of Robert Frost* edited by Edward Connery Lathem. Copyright 1956 by Robert Frost, © 1928, 1969, by Henry Holt and Company, LLC. Reprinted by permission of Henry Holt and Company, LLC. **(p. 53)**

IMG Literary. From *The Canadians* by Andrew Malcolm. Copyright © 1985. Reprinted by permission of IMG Literary. **(p. 7)**

Jen, Gish. From "The White Umbrella" by Gish Jen. Copyright © 1984 by Gish Jen. First published in *The Yale Review*. Reprinted by permission of the author. **(p. 41)**

Kinsella, W. P. From "Mankiewitz Won't Be Bowling Tuesday Nights Anymore" from *Shoeless Joe Jackson Comes to Iowa* by W. P. Kinsella. Reprinted by permission of W. P. Kinsella. **(p. 36)**

Kleiman, Carol. From "My Home Is Not Broken, It Works" by Carol Kleiman, 1984 as appeared in *Ms.* Magazine. Reprinted by permission of Carol Kleiman, Chicago Tribune Columnist and Contributing Editor to *Ms.* Magazine. **(p. 6)**

Ellen Levine Literary Agency, Inc. From *Fragments of The Ark*, published by Simon & Schuster. Reprinted by permission of Ellen Levine Literary Agency, Inc. Copyright © 1994 by Louise Meriwether. **(p. 81)**

Little, Brown and Company (Inc). From *Dream Makers, Dream Breakers: The World of Justice Thurgood Marshall* by Carl T. Rowan. Copyright © 1993 by CTR Productions, Inc. By permission of Little, Brown and Company (Inc). **(p. 4)**

LANGUAGE ARTS, READING

Name: _____ Class: _____ Date: _____

○ Simulated Test A   ○ Simulated Test B

1 ① ② ③ ④ ⑤   **11** ① ② ③ ④ ⑤   **21** ① ② ③ ④ ⑤   **31** ① ② ③ ④ ⑤

2 ① ② ③ ④ ⑤   **12** ① ② ③ ④ ⑤   **22** ① ② ③ ④ ⑤   **32** ① ② ③ ④ ⑤

3 ① ② ③ ④ ⑤   **13** ① ② ③ ④ ⑤   **23** ① ② ③ ④ ⑤   **33** ① ② ③ ④ ⑤

4 ① ② ③ ④ ⑤   **14** ① ② ③ ④ ⑤   **24** ① ② ③ ④ ⑤   **34** ① ② ③ ④ ⑤

5 ① ② ③ ④ ⑤   **15** ① ② ③ ④ ⑤   **25** ① ② ③ ④ ⑤   **35** ① ② ③ ④ ⑤

6 ① ② ③ ④ ⑤   **16** ① ② ③ ④ ⑤   **26** ① ② ③ ④ ⑤   **36** ① ② ③ ④ ⑤

7 ① ② ③ ④ ⑤   **17** ① ② ③ ④ ⑤   **27** ① ② ③ ④ ⑤   **37** ① ② ③ ④ ⑤

8 ① ② ③ ④ ⑤   **18** ① ② ③ ④ ⑤   **28** ① ② ③ ④ ⑤   **38** ① ② ③ ④ ⑤

9 ① ② ③ ④ ⑤   **19** ① ② ③ ④ ⑤   **29** ① ② ③ ④ ⑤   **39** ① ② ③ ④ ⑤

10 ① ② ③ ④ ⑤   **20** ① ② ③ ④ ⑤   **30** ① ② ③ ④ ⑤   **40** ① ② ③ ④ ⑤